PERESTROIKA:
GLOBAL CHALLENGE

OUR COMMON FUTURE

D0746643

Perestroika: Global Challenge

Our Common Future

Mikhail Gorbachev

Michael Barratt Brown, Keith and Anne Buchanan,
Luciana Castellina, Ken Coates, Andre Gunder Frank,
Stuart Holland, Marek Thee, Maarten van Traa and
Bob de Ruiter, Joop den Uyl, Norbert Wieczorek

Edited by **Ken Coates**

Introduced by the Rt. Hon **Neil Kinnock MP**

SPOKESMAN

First published in 1988 by:
Spokesman
Bertrand Russell House
Gamble Street
Nottingham, England
Tel. 0602 708318

British Library Cataloguing in Publication Data
Perestroika: the global challenge.
  1. Foreign relations. Crises. Management
  I. Coates, Ken, *1930-*
327.2

ISBN 0-85124-501-3
ISBN 0-85124-502-1 Pbk

Published by the Russell Press Ltd, Nottingham
(Tel. 0602 784505)

Contents

Perestroika:
The Global Challenge

An Introduction by the Rt. Hon Neil Kinnock MP

For over 40 years, East/West relations have been dominated by the Cold War. The thaw which seemed possible in some of Nikita Khrushchev's years became deep freeze again for most of the Brehznev era. Dubcek's 'socialism with a human face' was crushed under the tanks in August 1968 much as other struggles for autonomy in Hungary and elsewhere had been dealt with in the 1950s. The popular movement of Solidarnosc in 1981 was answered by a military dictatorship and seven years later troops are still the only answer that the system seems capable of giving to the struggle for negotiating rights. The Gulag, the Soviet intervention in Afghanistan and Moscow's hegemony over Eastern Europe gave proof that the spectre of Stalin still ruled.

In such a climate, only a few years ago, the idea that there could be a 'Moscow Spring' would have been dismissed as mere fantasy. The possibility that the Soviet leadership could and would challenge its own past and try to shape a genuine new future seemed utterly impossible.

It seemed out of the question that the Soviet leadership should come to regard conservatism in its own Party as one of the main obstacles to change; that democratisation should be set as one of the main objectives of policy or that new market relations should be set as a priority for economic policy. Anyone predicting that the Soviets would negotiate a deal to abolish INF weapons or welcome a 50 per cent cut in strategic weapons or seek to stimulate other arms reductions would have been dismissed as a dreamer.

Yet within only a few years since Mikhail Gorbachev became General Secretary of the Communist Party of the Soviet Union, much has changed. In part, this is because a new and younger leadership has replaced a gerontocracy. But *Perestroika* is more than a generational gear shift, more deliberate and detailed than any reform programme of the kind attempted by Khrushchev. And it represents therefore a challenge to us in the West to consider whether our stereotypes of the Soviets — fixed in more than four decades since uneasy wartime alliance became fierce peacetime hostility — are adequate for dealing with the new realities and profiting from the new opportunities.

Changes taking place in the Soviet Union demand both analysis and argument. They cannot and should not be taken simply at face value if they are to be properly understood and I strongly welcome, therefore, the range and depth of assessments made in this volume.

Plainly the new leadership in the Soviet Union places a high priority on economic development. It recognises that the worth of its system will in the long-run be measured not by its military might but by its capacity to meet the needs of the people.

It has undertaken to remove the rigidities and inefficiencies of the system. It has also made clear its dissatisfaction with the cost of the arms race and its fear both of the military threat posed by Star Wars and of the costs of either duplicating or circumventing it.

Having met Mikhail Gorbachev for several hours of direct conversation before he became General Secretary and having watched his statements and actions from the moment that he became Russian leader, I am not surprised by the direction that he wants to pursue. It is the pace and the audacity with which he has moved which has been unexpected.

No one now doubts his ability. No one should doubt his capacity to employ a breadth of vision and ambition or his equal readiness to use a geniality which is all the more convincing because it is natural.

Given all that, no one should fail to understand, either, that Mikhail Gorbachev is pre-eminently a Soviet Man. He owes everything that he has to the system and is proud and patriotic about it to the point of deeply resenting any outside criticism. In addition, he is a man who remembers seeing the Panzer divisions sweeping through his own village and he is determined that no incursion shall be made on the security of the Soviet Union or its dependents and allies.

Gorbachev's attitude towards the Soviet system is much more one of frustration at what he considers to be the failure to exploit its potential than criticism of its congenital inadequacies as an economic and political system.

His determination to rid the system of the people and attitudes which, to him, are the causes of that failure is complete. That slab of Soviet society which owes its senior and middle management comfort more to its willingness to conform to an established order than to merit or skill is the greatest barrier to change. Because it has a vested interest in immobility and because it is spread at vital levels through the decision-making (or not making) apparatus in industry, the bureaucracy, education and the military it has a negative strength of resistance. That conservative class must be changed or replaced if Gorbachev's version of *Perestroika* — of the reconstruction of the Soviet Union — is to advance with the speed and on the scale necessary to give Russia the chance of entering the 21st Century with vitality.

To secure such an alteration in the power structure of the myriad of institutions and agencies and offices and factories, Gorbachev needs resources for reconstruction as well as a will for reconstruction. He cannot get the combination of management and market, of planned investment in modernisation and provision for consumption if those resources are pre-empted by expenditure on the technology and staffing of military might — and he knows it.

If the pressure on the resources of the Soviet system that come from quantative and qualitative changes in the weapons and strategies of the Western Alliance (and the Chinese People's Republic) intensify, Gorbachev will still proceed with his attempts at managerial and industrial revolution. The problem is that he will do so in tension and with tension; the Alliance and all in the West should make their calculation about equilibrium, international relationships and the pace and implications of change in Russia in that knowledge.

Gorbachev is determined in any event to bring changes. If he can obtain the necessary resources he will do it in the rather genteel and progressive fashion that he prefers. Even if the social and political liberalisation of the Soviet Union did not surge forward in the way that democratic socialists would want, it would at least be significant and sustained and it would reflect economic development.

If there is a shortage of resources, however, Gorbachev will be less genteel and in place of encouragement and inducement he will use the powers of direction and discipline of which he is capable. That will still mean that he is the first Gorbachev and certainly not the second Stalin. But it will also mean that Russia has been merely altered rather than reconstructed.

Intensification of pressure on resources will not therefore forbid economic development or provoke economic collapse in Gorbachev's Russia. It will simply make the internal changes slower and more arduous and the external relations more brittle.

Neither can enhance the prospects for detente or arms build down or stability and neither will serve the defence or economic interests of the Western Alliance in general or Britain and Europe in particular.

So what policies towards the USSR will reduce confrontation, and what will increase it?

A strategy which sought to impose a new arms race on the USSR to 'spend them into the ground', is a strategy which will, inevitably, strengthen the hand of the authoritarians and conservatives. Their demands for internal control, for the continual allocation of money, technology and brains to the military effort, for the postponement of consumption and the denial of adequate investment to industry would be sustained. That can profit no-one but them and, perhaps, those who mirror their attitudes — if not their politics — in the West.

For most of the rest of us there is a better way. Without innocence but with determination, we can encourage and strengthen economic and political *Perestroika* in the knowledge that, whilst the military component of the East/West relationship will remain important for years to come, it can lose its primacy as the dominating determinant of all other relationships.

That isn't 'going soft' on the Soviets. It is saying that, if there are notable and proven intentions of the Russian leadership to move away from totalitarianism and all that implies for the Superpowers' internal and external conduct, the enemies of totalitarianism should do everything possible to assist that shift both in the interests of security and of liberty.

If the Soviet leadership wants to give priority to economic development, let us make it easier for it to divert funds from the military machine. We shall benefit in many ways from that, as much as they will.

If they have become gradually aware that they cannot indefinitely keep Eastern Europe captive, let us create incentives for them to relax their control — and certainly, let us not put the military pressure back on so they crash the prison doors shut again.

If they want to liberalise civil rights, let us act with a discretion that encourages them in the right direction, but leaves them the initiative to deal with their internal affairs. They will not, with such changes, make their system more tempting to people who know the superiorities of pluralist democracy. But they will develop a greater vested interest in prosperity and build a greater momentum for further liberalisation.

Besides, it is clear also that Mikhail Gorbachev aims not only at fundamental reforms within the Soviet Union, but also in Soviet relations with the wider world. For the first time since the war, the Soviet leadership is taking initiatives in both East/West and North/South relations.

This is evident not only from the dialogue which I and others have had with Gorbachev himself, nor only from his book *Perestroika: New Thinking for Our Country and for the World.* It also is especially clear from the statement on 'Realities and Guarantees for a Secure World' which Ken Coates has rightly highlighted in this volume.

In this statement Mikhail Gorbachev persistently stresses the importance of multilateral joint action through the United Nations both to maintain progress in disarmament, and to promote the international development crucial for North and South alike.

Thus he claims that unconditional observance of the United Nations charter, and the right of peoples to choose their own road to development — evolutionary or revolutionary — is an imperative condition for universal security. His concept for a widened role for the Security Council of the UN includes not only verification of arms control, but also that permanent members of the Council should become guarantors of regional security.

Joop den Uyl's proposals in this volume for reform of UN institutions very much complement the spirit of Gorbachev's initiative. Both on their merits, and in tribute to Joop himself, they should command attention and be widely discussed.

The same is true of the way in which Ken Coates addresses the need for a joint dialogue between people involved in the three inter-related constituencies of environment, development and peace.

Gro Harlem Brundtland's report last year to the Secretary General of the UN, *Our Common Future*, focused international attention on the need for a new model of environmental development. The economic committee of the Socialist International has stressed the imperative of linking priorities for the environment to specific measures in developing countries, such as debt relief. Likewise, Mikhail Gorbachev has introduced priority for protection of the environment in a series of statements which are unprecedented in recent Soviet history.

Clearly, the new Soviet concern for the environment postdates Chernobyl and exhortation is not the same thing as action. But, equally clearly, we should not dismiss the contribution which the Soviet Union, within a UN framework, could make towards realising some of the key objectives of the Brundtland report.

To say that much still remains to be done to make international *perestroika* real is to understate the size of the challenge. The Soviet Union has started withdrawal from Afghanistan, but still is involved in other theatres of conflict such as the Horn of Africa, where peace is a precondition of effective action to tackle the crisis stemming from drought, disease and deprivation. Yet the challenge has been made, unambiguously, within the UN framework. It is a proposal which we should take seriously — especially when Gorbachev has now built a record of validating words with actions.

Further, the Soviet leader has also declared the willingness of his country to play an active part in promoting a new world economic order. In his book *Perestroika,* he explicitly supports both the first and second Brandt Reports, *North/South* and *Common Crisis,* and the more recent Brandt/Manley *Global Challenge* report from the Socialist International.

In his own contribution to this volume, Stuart Holland — himself a contributor to the *Global Challenge* report — shows what this could mean in terms of new East/West and North/South co-operation, stressing realistically the difficulties which both the Soviet Union and the United States will need to surmount if progress is to be made in promoting a new development dialogue. Nonetheless, as with the originality shown by Gorbachev towards new roles for the United Nations, the opening for potential Soviet participation in joint action for development has been made, and is now on the international agenda.

Clearly, as illustrated by contributions to this volume, *Perestroika* is itself a challenge for the Soviet Union and not yet an accomplished fact. But it opens possibilities for co-operation rather than confrontation, for welfare rather than warfare, for both disarmament and detente that are so great that for once the word 'historic' is not an overstatement.

Lamentably, the Conservative Government in Britain has shown little readiness to recognise the scale of the challenge and the imperative of a positive response.

They — or at least their Leader — still consider that, in Bevan's words, 'it is easier to frame a military reply to the Soviet threat than a social and economic one' and would be more comfortable if such a simple choice could still be made. Realities are, however, too volatile for that. Consequently, we have a Prime Minister who feels that she has to give the impression of wanting to embrace the Bear on one day and of wanting to throttle it on the next.

These changes are not evidence of cunning perfidy. They are signs of someone not very sure of how to deal with change, when the General Secretary of the Communist Party of the Soviet Union takes productive initiatives, the President of the United States responds positively and leaders of Conservative European Governments understand and wish to exploit the new possibilities of change and co-existence.

We do not need to accept the new openness of *glasnost* or the reforms of *Perestroika* without reservation. We should not let slip our resolve to ensure that claims for progress are matched by progress in reality. The Berlin Wall still stands, public organisation or opposition in the Soviet Union still requires great nerve and tenacity, freedom to travel has not been achieved.

Yet if we are to make sure that we defend not only ourselves and our children, but also future generations, against the horrors of nuclear holocaust: if we are to offer people in the South a life at more than the margin of existence: if we are to gain common security in the common interest, it should be incumbent on us to address the challenge of *Perestroika* and also to respond at a range of levels, including action by governments, international agencies, informal meetings and other initiatives.

It is in such a context that I welcome the proposal for a Disarmament and Development Initiative by the Russell Foundation, published in this volume. Its aim, to bring together those in both the peace movements and the development lobbies in joint action to promote East/West and North/South co-operation, could play a significant role in responding to the challenge posed by *Perestroika* — and in intensifying the pressures for more of it.

I

Our
Common
Future

1: A Disarmament and Development Initiative for Our Common Future

Ken Coates

"There are more hungry people in the world today, than ever before in human history, and their numbers are growing. In 1980, there were 340 million people in 87 developing countries not getting enough calories to prevent stunted growth and serious health risks . . . the world bank predicts that these numbers are likely to go on growing".

Gro Harlem Brundtland, the Prime Minister of Norway, started out from facts like this in preparing her World Commission on the Environment, whose report, *Our Common Future*, was one of the most significant events of 1987. The experts of this Commission were aware that they were facing a global challenge. Human misery constitutes but one dimension of this challenge: or, it would be truer to say, constitutes but one dimension of this generation's experience of disorder. It is other generations, soon to arrive, who will experience the full consequences of our present misdeeds.

The worst victims of poverty are caught in a fearsome crisis of debt. But even those countries which are far above this threshold find they have mortgaged their future development in order to pay for their past expansion. Much of the debt of the South was incurred by military dictatorships. It is now imposed on new democracies. It is also worsened by high US interest rates which reflect the cost of the Strategic Defence Initiative and the biggest arms build-up in American peace-time history. This defence spending militates against development. If the debtors joined to exert combined bargaining power they could remedy this situation. For, as Keynes said, owing the bank £100 is your problem; owing it £1 million is the banker's problem. Now that developing countries owe well over $1 trillion it is a common problem for both the North and South which needs a joint international initiative to resolve it.

The world debt crisis accelerates the spoliation of natural resources. Irreplaceable rain forests are uprooted for quick profit, destroying whole species in the process. The elimination of species wastes inestimable resources laid up during the entire span of evolution. Millions of years of struggle and adjustment can be wiped away in order to secure a petty improvement in the value of exports. Who has time to weigh the balance of life when the creditor knocks? In Madagascar 93 per cent of the original forest has gone, and this means that probably 6,000 varieties of plants have been killed off. Each was once unique. Lake Malawi is being rapidly poisoned, imperilling the future of more than 500 species of fish. In Western Ecuador, almost all the primal forests have given way to plantations of bananas, or oil wells.

"The number of species thus eliminated . . . could well number 50,000 or more — all in just twenty-five years".

The wetlands of Brazil are similarly imperilled.

All this cutting and clearing, bulldozing and burning, contributes to profound atmospheric change culminating in what the scientists have styled "the greenhouse effect", briefly discussed by Luciana Castellina in the papers which follow. As the planet heats up, so future food production becomes more problematic. Before some of our grandchildren are thinking about their pensions, the icecaps will be melting, and the waters will be rising around our coastal plains and cities.

Of course, before 1987, many young people were by no means convinced that there was any chance that such problems would come to fruition, since it was widely supposed that an inevitable war would have carried off most human beings long before they had any time to evaluate the effects of this mess. But the Washington summit, for the first time ever, agreed on measures of real disarmament, actually removing an entire category of nuclear weapons from deployment. Modest though this measure of disarmament must be adjudged to be, when weighed against the vast accumulations of strategic missiles, none the less it represented a most significant shift in the assumptions of military planning. Hope was once again in order, and might just possibly become fashionable.

Two years before the Brundtland Commission announced its findings, the Socialist International had published its own *Global Challenge*, its first major report on international economic policy, presented under the auspices of Michael Manley and Willy Brandt. One of the contributors to this important statement was the British Labour Member of Parliament, Stuart Holland, who has submitted a key essay to this book. Messrs. Manley and Brandt set out a simple agenda:

"Our answer to militarism, monetarism and the transnational trend of trade and payments is clear. We need recovery and global spending, a restructuring of finance and trade, and a major redistribution of resources if we are to make possible a process of self-reinforcing, sustained social development into the twenty-first century".

None of this is easy. "At present", say the Socialist International's spokesmen, "it is blocked by some of the most powerfully vested interests in the world economy".

Why do we experience these warnings, one after another? Increasingly, they come from international teams of specialists, or political collaborators. It seems that, beneath the surface of these great difficulties in the management of the natural environment or the social economy there lies an even deeper crisis: the crisis of national democracy. Following the victory in the second world war, democratic advance had taken place over a very wide area of the world. Always imperfect, it was often ambiguous and sometimes badly flawed. But in the advanced countries, resting on two or three decades of relatively full employment, it provided a long expansion of broadly consensual constitutional development. During the same years, anti-colonial movements grew stronger and then triumphed, and their latest victories undermined the last centres of autocratic power in Europe.

The post-war economic arrangements which guaranteed stable expansion and a secure political consensus were also responsible for encouraging another development, however. They provided fertile soil for the growth of multinational capital, and thus launched business organization to a new level of power, unmatched by any purely national degree of sovereignty.

Multinational companies can run faster than the separate public health and conservation services of mere states. Macro-economic management is increasingly powerless at the national level, unless it follows directly on the trends determined in the interaction of global companies. Welfare infrastructures cannot find international linkages to enable them to escape the resultant national pressures for cuts and restrictions at every level. The grander big enterprise becomes, the shoddier the social fabric of education, health and welfare is likely to remain. In the poor countries debt and hunger rage. People are in open crisis. This is why, whichever way we turn, we now find that global problems present themselves, and reproach the inadequacies of our national democracies ever more keenly.

None of this process is confined to the capitalist democracies. A parallel development within the same world market has brought the Soviet Union and China to face the same global crisis. And that is why one of the most important attempts to explain the interconnections which are involved in this crisis was made by Mikhail Gorbachev, in his letter to the United Nations General

Assembly of August 1987. This was subsequently published in
Pravda on September 17th.

Here, Gorbachev was taking the theme of his democratic
restructuring in the Soviet Union itself, *Perestroika*, and applying it
to the international institutions which are the only inadequate
existing mechanisms through which co-operation might be
organized at anything like an appropriate scale. Over decades, the
majority of nations have agreed on the need for a new international
economic order. The Socialist Parties of Western Europe and Latin
America are welcome supporters of this call, but they were by no
means the first to launch it. Before them, the non-aligned states had
agreed extensive proposals, designed to protect their interest in the
outcome. The explosion of international debt has underlined the
need for co-ordinated action, without providing any half-way to
adequate machinery through which it could be organized.

Political will in the modern world is formed in accordance with
national interests expressed through national organizations and
shaped by states. How can we possibly arouse a proper response to
world-wide issues if we cannot begin to transcend these limitations
of our given political structures?

Evidently, Perestroika is one thing. The Global Challenge is
another, which obtained the support of more than its core 84
Parties. *Our Common Future* sought to distill its findings from a
whole directory of scientists and specialists scattered all around the
planet, but it is only necessary to perceive the vastness of the tasks
which it seeks to confront in order to realize the scope of the joint
action that will be needed if this is to be done.

Linkage between all these separate initiatives seems
indispensable to the success of any one of them. The closer the
linkage, the greater reinforcement of success.

With this aim in mind, the Russell Foundation circulated Mikhail
Gorbachev's appeal among a number of concerned parties, to invite
their responses on the various items of its agenda. At the same time,
we have been seeking support for a joint initiative which might link
the issues of disarmament and development, underpinning both in
the process. Supposing that the separate platforms of Global
Challenge and Perestroika could be joined together, and the issue
of the protection of the planetary environment could be linked to
the development of a secure human future: would we not stand at
the beginning of a new alliance of the world's democrats?

Without such an alliance, does anybody imagine that it might be
possible to muddle our way into the next century? Or to survive the
cosmic mess we are daily making if we did? In the hope of helping to
focus discussion on the need for just such an alliance, the Bertrand
Russell Peace Foundation has been circulating the text of an appeal

for a Disarmament and Development Initiative (DDI). We would welcome support for its statement, which is as follows:

The Disarmament and Development Initiative (DDI)
The 1970s and 1980s have been dominated by two overpowering questions. First, there has been a crisis in militarism, expressed in a runaway arms race which, until very recently, appeared to be impossible to restrain.

During the same years, monetarism and economic recession ended the postwar Keynesian world settlement. In the developed world, unemployment rose continuously with severe structural decline in many countries, promoting grave social tensions.

Yet, in 1987, the world witnessed a giant step forward to meet the needs of the agenda of disarmament, with an agreement in principle to remove intermediate nuclear forces from deployment in Europe and Asia. The agreement has brought hope to humanity that the nuclear arms race not only can be stopped, but actually reversed. The superpowers, who could cry "havoc" have in fact cried "halt" in the most over-armed theatres in the world. Credit is due to both sides for this historic accord.

The INF agreement is more than a "window" of opportunity. But it is crowded by other pressures and other conflicts which feed the demand for more arms. The Iran/Iraq war threatens the stability of the Middle East, with increasing involvement by the United States and European powers. The Soviet Union still is not extricated from Afghanistan. The African and Asian Sub-continents are rent with wars which lacerate their peoples and their prospects for development.

Apart from other nuclear weapons, the SDI or Star Wars project still feeds the military industrial complex in the United States. The stockpiles of chemical and biological weapons have not yet been abolished. Massive conventional forces are still deployed in the first, second and third worlds alike — pre-empting civil expenditure on housing, health, education and social services.

The Warfare state militates against a global Welfare Society. In the words of Willy Brandt the world at present is "arming itself to death". Monetarism and militarism walk hand in hand. Governments offset slow growth with sustained or increased arms spending. Since the 1973 and 1979 oil price increases the monetarists have offered panaceas for global welfare: float exchange rates, free financial markets, cut public spending and dismantle the welfare state.

Yet, fifteen years on, the world economy is disintegrating. Devaluation will not remedy the payments deficits of the United States and the United Kingdom. But these deficits are indications of trouble to come for other important currencies. The Casino economy against which Keynes railed is now worldwide. Whereas ten years ago 85 per cent of foreign exchange transactions were to finance trade, the same share today feeds currency speculation.

Meanwhile, Africa is wracked by drought, disease, debt and deprivation.

Latin America is deep in crisis with unpayable debts and cuts in trade and living standards which threaten the stability of its new democracies.

Beggar-my-neighbour protection is on the agenda of GATT. But it is beggar-my-neighbour deflation, and the paralysis it brings to trade which is crippling the south, while the north slow burns with persistently high unemployment.

If the United States administration does cut its deficit by restraint, including arms cuts, to achieve a balanced budget by 1993, this could mean negative growth by that year in Latin America and Europe, increasing Western Europe's unemployment to twenty-four million.

The growth of trade between the Soviet Union and Eastern Europe and the rest of the world could fall nearly five-fold, to only half of one per cent a year. Trade and debt turbulence would threaten the collapse of the already insecure global trade and payment system.

It is for such reasons that we must offset reduced arms spending and support disarmament with increased development expenditure. We need to reverse beggar-my-neighbour policies with better-my-neighbour strategies aimed to:

1. Recover mutual spending and production — including public and social expenditure — and thus increase import and export trade, jobs and incomes;
2. Restructure power relations between North and South, East and West, with a rescheduling and writing down of the debt which inhibits development itself;
3. Redistribute demand towards those in the South who need it most, with beneficial effects on their own economies and welfare, and also on exports and jobs in the north.

In effect, we need to offset *militarism* and *monetarism* by new policies, both on *disarmament* and *development*.

The prototypes for such a genuinely new international order have been blueprinted by a range of reports, including those from the Brandt Commission (*North South and Common Crisis*, Pan Books), as well as the *Out of Crisis* project (Spokesman) co-ordinated by the British politician Stuart Holland, which prototyped the '3R' case for Recovery, Restructuring and Redistribution, echoed and developed in the North South and East

West context by the Brandt-Manley *Global Challenge* report from the Socialist International.

Links between debt, deprivation and inability to protect the world's environment have been highlighted by the recent report, *Our Common Future*, chaired by Gro Harlem Brundtland (Oxford University Press). Likewise, the Palme Commission made specific proposals for extending nuclear-free zones to zones free from conventional weapons in Central Europe (*Common Security*, Pan Books).

More recently, in a series of audacious initiatives, Mikhail Gorbachev related the concepts of military and economic security. The Chinese authorities have shown real interest in new forms of international co-operation — including the Global Challenge Report — as have other key countries among the non-aligned, such as India, Yugoslavia and Brazil.

It is imperative to extend such initiatives combining disarmament and development to a new level at which wider public pressure and participation can both support and advance such change.

The international peace movement — and the recent response to Band Aid, Live Aid and Sport Aid — have shown millions of people worldwide how to mobilize mass support for disarmament and development. But hitherto, even when they have drawn support from the same people, these causes have remained separate. We must bring them together, because unless the world is made fit for its peoples to live in, peace will always be in jeopardy: and while the world's treasure is wasted on war preparations, poverty and distress will always recur. Crisis not only engenders hunger: it undermines democracy where it already exists, and inhibits its development elsewhere. Even in countries which have abandoned capitalist forms of organization, the impact of crisis can be felt. Nothing could more gravely impede the existing programme of economic and democratic reform in the two most powerful Communist countries than the pressures of a world economy slithering from depression into slump.

This implies the need for a new initiative: a Disarmament and Development Initiative (DDI) as opposed to the threat of the Strategic Defence Initiative (SDI).

We have decided to seek general support for such a proposal. We would greatly value your criticism and advice, and also your help in persuading either individuals or organizations to offer their assistance. We are looking for aid in promoting a series of relevant seminars on particular questions, both nationally and internationally. We also seek to reach towards the possibility of joint action, practical collaboration, to bring such an initiative to life.

II

Perestroika:
Global
Challenge

2: Underpinning a Secure World*

Mikhail Gorbachev

The 42nd session of the United Nations General Assembly opened a few days ago. That fact suggested this article.

Objective processes are making our complex and diverse world more and more interrelated and interdependent. And it increasingly needs a mechanism capable of discussing common problems in a responsible fashion and at a representative level and mutually searching for a balance of differing, contradictory, yet real, interests of the contemporary community of states and nations. The United Nations Organisation is called upon to be such a mechanism by its underlying idea and its origin. We are confident that it is capable of fulfilling that role. This is why in the first days of autumn, when the holiday period is over and international political life is rapidly gathering momentum, when an opportunity for important decisions in the disarmament field can be discerned, we, in the Soviet leadership, deemed it useful to share our ideas on the basic issues of world politics at the end of the 20th century. It seems all the more appropriate since the current session of the United Nations General Assembly is devoted to major aspects of such politics.

It is natural that what we would like to do first of all in this connection is to try and see for ourselves what the idea of a comprehensive system of international security — the idea advanced at the 27th CPSU Congress — looks like 18 months after the Congress. This idea has won backing from many states. Our friends — the socialist countries and members of the non-aligned movement — are active co-authors.

The article offered to you deals primarily with our approach to the formation of such a system. At the same time it is an invitation for the United Nations member countries and the world public to exchange views.

*Published in *Pravda* on 17th September 1987 under the title: 'The Reality and Guarantees of a Secure World'.

I

The last quarter of the 20th century has brought changes in the material aspect of being — changes revolutionary in their content and significance. For the first time in its history mankind became capable of resolving many problems that hindered its progress over centuries. From the standpoint of the existing and newly-created resources and technologies, there are no impediments to feeding a population of many billions, to educating, it, providing it with housing and keeping it healthy. Given the obvious differences and potentialities of the various peoples and countries, a prospect has formed of befitting living conditions for the inhabitants of the Earth.

At the same time dangers have emerged which put into question the very immortality of the human race. This is why new rules of coexistence on our unique planet are badly needed and they should conform to the new requirements and the changed conditions.

Alas, many influential forces continue adhering to outdated notions concerning ways for ensuring national security. As a result the world is in an absurd situation with persistent efforts being made to convince it that the road to the abyss is the most correct one. It would be difficult to appraise in any other way the point of view that nuclear weapons make it possible to avert a world war. It is not simple to refute it precisely because it is totally unfounded. For one has to dispute something which is being passed off as an axiom — that since no world war has broken out after the emergence of nuclear weapons, those weapons have averted it. It would seem more correct to say that a world war has been averted despite the existence of nuclear weapons.

Some time back the sides had several scores of atomic bombs apiece, then each came to possess a hundred nuclear missiles, and finally, the arsenals grew to several thousand nuclear warheads. Not so long ago Soviet and American scientists made a special study of the relationship between strategic stability and the size of nuclear arsenals. They arrived at the unanimous conclusion that 95 per cent of all US and Soviet nuclear arms can be eliminated without stability being disrupted. This is a killing argument against the nuclear deterrence stategy, a strategy that gives birth to a mad logic. We believe that the 5 per cent should not be retained either. And then the stability will be qualitatively different.

Not laying claims to instructing anyone and having come to realise that mere statements about the dangerous situation in the world are unproductive, we began seeking an answer to the question of whether it was possible today to have a model ensuring national security which would not be fraught with the threat of a world-wide catastrophe.

Such an approach was in the mainstream of the concepts formed during the evolution of a new mode of political thinking permeated with a realistic view of what is surrounding us and what is happening around, of ourselves; this view is characterised by an unbiassed attitude to others and awareness of our own responsibility and security.

The new thinking is also bridging the gap between word and deed. And we have embarked on practical action. Sure that nuclear weapons are the greatest evil and pose the most horrible threat we announced a unilateral moratorium on nuclear tests which we observed, let me put it straight, longer than we might have done . . . Then came the January 15, 1986 Statement putting forth a concrete programme for stage-by-stage elimination of nuclear weapons. At the meeting with President Reagan in Reykjavik we came close to realisation of the desirability and possibility of complete nuclear disarmament. And then we made steps facilitating approach to an agreement on the elimination of two classes of nuclear arms — medium- and shorter-range missiles.

We believe such an agreement is possible and realistic. In this connection I would like to note that the Government of Federal Germany has assumed a stand conducive to this, to a certain extent. The Soviet Union is proceeding from the premise that a relevant treaty could be worked out before the end of the current year. Much has been said about its potential advantages. I will not repeat them. I would only like to note that it would deal a tangible blow at concepts of limited use of nuclear weapons and the so-called "controllable escalation" of a nuclear conflict. There are no illusory intermediate options. The situation is becoming more stable.

This treaty on medium- and shorter-range missiles would be a fine prelude to a breakthrough at the talks on large-scale — 50 per cent — reductions in strategic offensive arms in conditions of the strict observance of the ABM Treaty. I believe that, given the mutual striving, an accord on that matter could become a reality as early as the first half of next year.

While thinking of advancing towards a nuclear-weapon-free world it is essential to see to it even now that security be ensured in the process of disarmament, at each of its stages, and to think not only about that, but also to agree on mechanisms for maintaining peace at drastically reduced levels of non-nuclear armaments.

All these questions were included in proposals set forth jointly by the USSR and other socialist countries at the United Nations — proposals for the establishment of a comprehensive system of international peace and security.

How do we see it?

The security plan proposed by us provides, above all, for continuity and concord with the existing institutions for the maintenance of peace. The system could function on the basis of the UN Charter and within the framework of the United Nations. In our view, its ability to function will be ensured by the strict observance of the Charter's demands, additional unilateral obligations of states as well as confidence measures and international cooperation in all spheres — military-political, economic, ecological, humanitarian and others.

I do not venture to foretell how the system of all-embracing security would appear in its final form. It is only clear that this could become a reality only if all means of mass annihilation were destroyed. We propose that all this be pondered by an independent commission of experts and specialists, which would submit its conclusions to the United Nations Organisation.

Personally, I have no doubt about the capability of sovereign states to assume obligations in the field of international security already. Many states are doing this now. The Soviet Union and the People's Republic of China have stated that they will not be the first to use nuclear arms. The Soviet-American agreements on nuclear armaments are another example. They contain a conscious choice of restraint and self-limitation in the most sensitive sphere of relations between the USSR and the United States. Or take the Nuclear Non-Proliferation Treaty. What is it? It is a unique example of a high sense of responsibility of states.

In the present-day reality there already exist "bricks" from which one can start building the future system of security.

The sphere of the reasonable, responsible and rational organisation of international affairs is expanding before our very eyes, though admittedly timidly. Previously unknown standards of openness, of scope and depth for mutual control and verification of compliance with adopted obligations, are being established. An American inspection team has visited an area where exercises of Soviet troops were held; a group of United States Congressmen has inspected the Krasnoyarsk radar station; American scientists have installed and adjusted instruments in the area of the Soviet nuclear testing range. Soviet and American observers attend each other's military exercises. Annual plans of military activity are published under accords within the framework of the Helsinki process.

I do not know a weightier and more impressive argument in support of the fact that the situation is changing than the stated readiness of a nuclear power to voluntarily renounce nuclear weapons. References to an aspiration to replace them with conventional armaments in which there supposedly exists a disbalance between NATO and the Warsaw Treaty in the latter's favour are unjustified. If a disbalance and disproportions exist, let us remove them. We do not tire of saying this and we have proposed concrete ways of solving this problem.

In all these issues the Soviet Union is a pioneer and shows that its words are matched by deeds.

The question of comparing defence spending? Here we will have to put in more work. I think that, given proper effort, within the next two or three years we will be able to compare the figures that are of interest to us and our partners and which would symmetrically reflect the expenditures of all concerned.

The Soviet-American talks on nuclear and space arms, and a convention on the prohibition of chemical weapons which is close to being concluded will intensify, I am sure, the advance to detente and disarmament.

An accord on "defence strategy" and "military sufficiency" could impart a powerful impulse in this direction. These notions presuppose such a structure for the armed forces of a state as would make these forces sufficient for repulsing any possible aggression but inadequate for conducting offensive actions. The first step towards this could be a controlled withdrawal of nuclear and other offensive weapons from the borders with subsequent creation along borders of strips of reduced armaments and demilitarised zones between potential, let us put it this way, adversaries. While in principle we should work for the dissolution of military blocs and the liquidation of bases on foreign territory and the return home of all troops stationed abroad.

The question of a possible mechanism to prevent the outbreak of a nuclear conflict is more complex. Here I approach the most sensitive point of the idea of all-embracing security: much will have to be additionally pondered, rethought and improved. In any case, the international community should work out agreed upon measures for the event of violation of the all-embracing agreement on the non-use and elimination of nuclear arms or an attempt to violate this agreement. As to potential nuclear piracy, it appears possible and necessary to consider in advance and prepare collective measures to prevent it.

If the system is sufficiently effective, then it will provide even more effective guarantees of averting and curbing non-nuclear aggression.

The system proposed by us precisely presupposes definite measures to enable the United Nations, the main universal security body, to ensure the maintenance of security at a level of reliability.

II

The division of the world's countries into those possessing nuclear weapons and those not possessing them has split also the very concept of security. But for human life security is indivisible. In this sense it is not only a political, military, juridical but also a moral category. And contentions that there has been no war for already half a century do not withstand any test on the touchstone of ethics. How come there is no war? There are dozens of regional wars flaring up in the world!

It is immoral to treat this as something second rate. The point, though, lies not only in impermissible nuclear haughtiness. The elimination of nuclear weapons would also be a major step towards a genuine democratisation of relations between states, they being equal and bearing equal responsibility.

Unconditional observance of the United Nations Charter and the right of peoples to sovereignly choose the roads and forms of their development, revolutionary or evolutionary; is an imperative condition for universal security. This applies also to the right to a social status quo which is exclusively an internal matter. Any attempts, direct or indirect, to influence the development of countries "other than our own", to interfere in such development, should be ruled out. Just as inadmissible are attempts to destabilise existing governments from outside.

At the same time, the world community cannot stay away from interstate conflicts. Here it could be possible to begin by fulfilling the proposal made by the United Nations Secretary-General to set up under the United Nations Organisation a multilateral centre for lessening the danger of war. Evidently, it would be worth considering the expediency of setting up a direct communication line between the United Nations Headquarters and the capitals of the countries that are permanent members of the Security Council, and the location of the chairman of the non-aligned movement.

It appears to us that, with the aim of greater trust and mutual understanding, a mechanism could be set up under the aegis of the United Nations Organisation for extensive international verification of compliances with agreements to lessen international tension, limit armaments, and for monitoring the military situation in conflict areas. The mechanism would function via various forms and methods of monitoring to collect information and promptly submit it to the United Nations. This would provide an objective picture of the events taking place, and of sudden attacks, effectuation of measures to avert any armed conflict, and prevent such from expanding and becoming worse.

We are arriving at the conclusion that wider use should be made of the institution of United Nations military observers and United Nations peace-keeping forces in disengaging the troops of warring sides, observing cease-fire and armistice agreements.

And, of course, at all stages of a conflict extensive use should be made of all means for peaceful settlement of disputes and differences between states and one should offer good offices, and mediation with the aim of achieving an armistice. The ideas and initiatives concerning non-governmental commissions and groups which would analyse the causes, circumstances and methods of resolving various concrete conflict situations appear to be fruitful.

The Security Council permanent members could become guarantors of regional security. They could, on their part, assume an obligation not to use force or the threat of force, and could renounce demonstrative military presence, because such a practice is one of the factors fanning regional conflicts.

A drastic intensification and expansion of cooperation between states in uprooting international terrorism is extremely important. It would be expedient to concentrate this cooperation within the framework of the United Nations Organisation. In our opinion, it would be useful to create under its aegis a tribunal to investigate acts of international terrorism.

More coordination in the struggle against apartheid as a destabilising factor of international magnitude would also be justified.

As we see it, all the above-stated measures could be organically built into an all-embracing system for peace and security.

III

The events and tendencies of the past decades have expanded this concept, imparting new features and specificities to it. One of them is the problem of economic security. A world in which a whole continent can find itself on the brink of death from starvation and in which huge masses of people are suffering almost permanent malnutrition is not a safe world. Neither is a world safe in which a multitude of countries and peoples are being strangled in a noose of debt.

The economic interests of individual countries or their groups are indeed so different and contradictory that consensus with regard to the concept of a new world economic order seems hard to achieve. We do hope, however, that the instinct of self-preservation will snap into action here as well. It is sure to manifest itself if we succeed in examining the chain of priorities and seeing that there are circumstances, "menacing in their inevitability", and that it is time for abandoning an inert political mentality, and views of the outside world inherited from the past. This world has ceased to be a sphere which the big and strong divided into domains and zones of "vital interests".

The imperatives of the times compel us to institutionalise many common sense notions. It is not philanthropy which prompted our proposal for reduction in interest payments under bank credits and the elaboration of extra benefits for the least developed nations. This holds benefit for all, namely a secure future. If the debt burden of the developing world is alleviated, the chances for such a future will grow. It is also possible to limit debt payments by each developing country to a share of its annual export earnings without detriment to development; accept export commodities in payment for the debt; remove protectionist barriers on the borders of creditor-nations; and stop adding extra interest when deferring payments under debts.

There may be different attitudes to these proposals. There is no doubt, however, that the majority of international community members realise the need for immediate actions to ease the developing world's debt burden. If that is so, it is possible to start working out a programme through concerted effort.

The words "through concerted effort" are very important for today's world. The relationship between disarmament and development, confirmed at the recent international conference in New York, can be implemented if none of the strong and the rich keep themselves aloof. I have already expressed the view that Security Council member states, represented by their top officials, could jointly discuss this problem and work out a coordinated approach. I confirm this proposal.

Ecological security. It is not secure in the direct meaning of the word when currents of poison flow along river channels, when poisonous rains pour down from the sky, when an atmosphere polluted with industrial and transport waste chokes cities and whole regions, when the development of atomic engineering is accompanied by unacceptable risks.

Many have suddenly begun to perceive all these things not as something abstract, but as quite a real part of their own experience. The confidence that "this won't affect us", characteristic of the past outlook, has disappeared. They say that one thorn of experience is worth more than a whole forest of instructions. For us, Chernobyl became such a thorn . . .

The relationship between man and the environment has become menacing. Problems of ecological security affect all — the rich and the poor. What is required is a global strategy for environmental protection and the rational use of resources. We suggest starting its elaboration within the framework of a UN special programme.

States are already exchanging relevant information and notifying international organisations of developments. We believe that this order should be legitimised by introducing the principle of annual reports by governments about their conservationist activity and about ecological accidents, both those that have already occurred and those that were prevented on the territory of their countries.

Realising the need for opening a common front of economic and ecological security and starting its formation mean defusing a delayed-action bomb planted deep inside mankind's existence by history, by people themselves.

IV

Human rights. One can name all the top statesmen of our times who threatened to use nuclear weapons. Some may object: it is one thing to threaten and another to use. Indeed, they haven't used them. But campaigning for human rights is in no way compatible with the threat to use weapons of mass destruction. We hold it unacceptable to talk about human rights and liberties while intending to hang in outer space overhead the "chandeliers" of exotic weapons. The only down-to-earth element in that "exoticism" is the potentiality of mankind's annihilation. The rest is in dazzling wrapping.

I agree: the world cannot be considered secure if human rights are violated in it and, I will add, if a large part of this world has no elementary conditions for a life worthy of man, if millions of people have a full "right" to go hungry, to have no roof over their heads and to be jobless and sick indefinitely when treatment is something they cannot afford, if, finally, the most basic human right, the right to live, is disregarded.

First of all, it is necessary that everywhere national legislation and administrative rules in the humanitarian sphere as well be brought into accordance with international obligations and standards.

Simultaneously, it would be possible to turn to coordinating a broad selection of practical steps, for instance, to working out a world information programme under the UN auspices to familiarise peoples with one another's life, life as it is and not as someone would like to present it. That is precisely why such a project should envisage ridding the flow of information of "enemy image" stereotypes, of bias, prejudices and absurd concoctions, of deliberate distortion and unscrupulous violation of the truth.

There is much promise in the task of coordinating unified international legal criteria for handling in the humanitarian spirit issues of reunion of families, marriages, contacts between people and organisations, visa regulations and so on. What has been achieved on this account within the framework of the all-European process should be accepted as a starting point.

We favour the establishment of a special fund of humanitarian cooperation of the United Nations formed from voluntary state and private contributions through reductions in military spending.

It is advisable that all states join the UNESCO conventions in the sphere of culture, including the conventions on protection of the world cultural heritage, on prohibition and prevention of the illicit import, export and transfer of ownership of cultural property.

The alarming signals of recent times have pushed to the top of the agenda the idea of creating a world-wide network of medical cooperation in treating the most dangerous diseases, including AIDS, and combating drug addition and alcoholism. The existing structures of the World Health Organisation make it possible to establish such a network at relatively short notice. The leaders of the world movement of physicians have big ideas about this.

Dialogue on humanitarian problems could be conducted on a bilateral basis, within the forms of negotiation that have already been established. Besides, we propose holding such dialogue within the framework of an international conference in Moscow: we made that proposal at the Vienna meeting in November last year.

Pooling efforts in the sphere of culture, medicine and humanitarian rights is yet another integral part of the system of comprehensive security.

V

The suggested system of comprehensive security will be effective to the extent to which the United Nations, its Security Council and other international institutes and mechanisms will effectively function. It will be required to enhance resolutely the authority and role of the UN, and the International Atomic Energy Agency. The need for a world space organisation is clear. It could work in the future in close contact with the UN as an autonomous part of its system. UN specialised agencies should also become regulators of international processes. The Geneva Conference on Disarmament should become a forum that would internationalise the transition to a nuclear-free, non-violent world.

One should not forget the capacities of the International Court either. The General Assembly and the Security Council could approach it more often for consultative conclusions on international disputes. Its mandatory jurisdiction should be recognised by all on mutually agreed upon conditions. The permanent members of the Security Council, due to their special responsibility, should take the first step in that direction.

We are convinced that a comprehensive system of security is at the same time a system of universal law and order ensuring the primacy of international law in politics.

The UN Charter gives extensive powers to the Security Council. Joint efforts are required to ensure that it could use them effectively. For this purpose, there would be sense in holding meetings of the Security Council at foreign ministers' level when opening a regular session of the General Assembly to review the international situation and jointly look for effective ways towards improvement.

It would be useful to hold meetings of the Security Council not only at the headquarters of the UN in New York, but also in regions of friction and tension and alternate them among the capitals of the permanent member states.

Special missions of the Council to regions of actual and potential conflicts would also help consolidate its authority and enhance the effectiveness of decisions adopted.

We are convinced that cooperation between the UN and regional organisations could be considerably expanded. Its aim is the search for a political settlement to crisis situations.

In our view, it is important to hold special sessions of the General Assembly on the more urgent political problems and individual disarmament issues more often if the efficiency of the latter's work is to be improved.

We emphatically stress the need for making the status of important political documents passed at the United Nations by consensus more binding morally and politically. Let me recall that they include, among others, the final document of the 1st Special Session of the United Nations General Assembly devoted to disarmament, and the Charter of Economic Rights and Obligations of States.

In our opinion, we should have long since set up a world consultative council under the UN auspices to bring together the world's intellectual elite. Prominent scientists, political and public figures, representatives of international public organisations, cultural workers, people in literature and the arts, including laureates of the Nobel Prize and other international prizes of world-wide significance, and eminent representatives of the churches, could seriously enrich the spiritual and ethical potential of contemporary world politics.

To ensure that the United Nations and its specialised agencies operate at full capacity one should come to realise that it is impermissible to use financial levers to pressure it. The Soviet Union will continue to cooperate actively in overcoming budget difficulties arising at the United Nations.

And, finally, as regards the United Nations Secretary-General. The international community elects to that high post an authoritative figure who enjoys everybody's trust. Since the

Secretary-General is functioning as a representative of every
member country of the organisation, all states should give him
maximum support and help him in fulfiling his responsible mission.
The international community should encourage the United Nations
Secretary-General in his missions of good offices, mediation and
reconciliation.

*   *   *

Why are we so persistent in raising the question of a comprehensive
system of international peace and security?

Simply because it is impossible to put up with the situation in
which the world has found itself as the third millennium draws nigh
— in the face of a threat of annihilation, in a state of constant
tension, in an atmosphere of suspicion and strife, spending huge
funds and quantities of work and talent by millions of people only to
increase mutual distrust and fears.

We can speak till we are blue in the face about the need for
terminating the arms race, uprooting militarism, or about
cooperation. Nothing will change unless we start acting.

The political and moral core of the problem is the trust of states
and peoples in one another, respect for international agreements
and institutions. And we are prepared to switch from confidence
measures in individual spheres to a large-scale policy of trust which
would gradually shape a system of comprehensive security. But
such a policy should be based on community of political statements
and real positions.

The idea of a comprehensive system of security is the first plan for
a possible new organisation of life in our common planetary home.
In other words, it is a ticket into a future where security for all is a
token of the security for everyone. We hope that the current session
of the United Nations General Assembly will jointly develop and
concretise this idea.

3: Economic Security

Michael Barratt Brown

Introduction

Secretary-General Gorbachev last September presented to the United Nations general assembly a major statement on "The Reality and the Guarantees of a Secure World". In this he made a special point of the relationship between Disarmament and Development. A world he said, in which "whole continents are on the brink of starvation" and "others caught in a noose of debt" cannot be a safe world. At the same time funds released from military spending could be applied to humanitarian cooperation. Perhaps most strikingly, Mr. Gorbachev challenged the concept of the world as one which "the big and the strong divide into domains and zones of 'vital interests'". Apart from the military implications of this statement, the economic implications are very great. The appeal for joint action both to alleviate hunger and debt and to secure the ecological environment demand a most thoughtful response. In this paper I propose to respond to the issue of economic security. Others will take up the ecological issue.

The Nature of Economic Insecurity

Security is a big strong word. It is what everyone wants. The man of property wants his property secure; the householder her house secure; the worker his job secure; the peasant her crop secure; the starving the next meal secure; the homeless their shelter secure. We all want a secure peace and we are beginning to learn that this can no longer be at the expense of someone else's insecurity. Military security is no longer divisible. But what about economic security? It is just possible for some to have it at the expense of others, but only just. As the spread of nuclear fall-out can envelop the whole world, so the spread of the debt fall-out could hardly leave anyone untouched, certainly not the bankers of the industrialised countries. Unfortunately, there is a cross dysfunction: the nuclear threat, if it remains a threat, does benefit a few who make the nuclear arms, while the economic crisis does affect all, although some much more than others.

It is clear enough that economic insecurity and military insecurity are mutually interactive. Each generates and aggravates the other. Economic insecurity is a powerful generator of military regimes and of attempted military solutions to problems. At the same time, the arms race — a race to achieve a supposed military security — preempts resources which might have been used for improving economic security, and not only in the poor countries. United States congressman Mekhon observed some years ago that "Nothing will hearten a potential opponent more than to observe we lead the country into bankruptcy and destroy the economy, while ensuring over many years our full preparedness for military conflict." It is a matter of some importance that the original line of causation seems to run from the economic to the military. Whether it is the need of the giant companies to find markets for overproduction and opportunities for flagging investment or the need of governments to find a distraction from economic failures and inequalities of wealth, the economic cause appears to be primary. If this is correct, it means that the current world-wide economic insecurity bodes ill for the peace of the world. It is generally accepted that it was the world economic crisis and slump of the 1930s that created the conditions for fascism and for the outbreak of the Second World War. Humanity cannot hope to survive a Third World War.

1930 and 1988 compared
How was it that the Wall Street stock exchange crash of October 1929 led so inexorably to depression and war? What can be done to prevent a re-run of those events after the crash of October 1987? First results are no indicator. There was no immediate decline in world trade, in output or employment after the crash of 1929. The decline began in mid-1930 and accelerated downwards in 1931 and right through to 1939, recovery beginning hesitantly only in 1933. By mid-1933 the value, of world trade had been halved, industrial output reduced by a third, unemployment raised in the USA from 3% to 25% and in Britain from 10% to 22%, with Stock Exchange prices in both countries at a quarter of their 1929 heights.

The fact is that the boom that preceded the crash both 1987 and 1929 was not just a speculative boom, which could then be expected to correct itself. The speculation itself in both cases arose from the growing inequality of incomes, the rich investing their higher incomes in the Stock Market and living on credit, which they could repay from higher stock values, and the poor unable to buy products of the new investments as their real income were eroded by inflation. What happens after a crash is that the rich reduce their spending and cut back on their use of credit. Demand for goods and services are reduced, factories are closed down, investment is cut back and more and more unemployed are reduced to the ranks of the poor. It needs to be recognised that, while in 1929 there were only 1.5 million Americans with Stock Exchange accounts, by 1987 there were 48 million — more than a quarter of the adult population. In Britain Thatcher's popular capitalism has raised the number who own shares from 2½ million to 8½ million, a fifth of the population. When such a proportion of the more affluent part of the population starts to cut back on spending, even if they increase their saving, the result must be recessionary. The motor traders already expect to sell a quarter of a million less cars in the British market in 1988 than they sold in 1987.

The slump of the early 1930s hit hardest the primary producers, not only the Okies of John Steinbeck's *Grapes of Wrath*, but food and raw material producers throughout the Third World. They could less easily protect themselves against price falls than the manufacturers. Primary product prices on average fell by more than a half. This meant that if you kept your job in the USA or in the UK, you could actually benefit from cheaper food. Today protectionist measures in the USA and in the European Community are keeping up their food prices, but this does not benefit the Third World. In the 1930's the ruin of the primary producers in the Third World meant that they bought less from the industrial countries, so that unemployment multiplied there too. It will be the same today. A vicious downward spiral developed in the 1930s made worse by the protectionist policies of the industrial countries. Beggar-my-neighbour was the order of the day among the rival powers who sought to hold or capture colonial markets where they could. It is beginning to be the same today. On top of the massive protection of the European agricultural market the United States is seeking to protect its markets. Japan has always been protectionist. Worse still today is the beggar-my-neighbour of economic deflation which by reducing purchasing power at home seeks to reduce imports and to expand exports. For, if all countries follow suit then the whole level of world trade is reduced.

In this situation the old pattern of spheres of influence is re-emerging. Such spheres of influence in the past have been based on areas of economic interest and political control by the great powers. We can distinguish, after the early Spanish, Portuguese and Dutch empires, the British Empire and subsequent Sterling Area, the United States 'Manifest Destiny' in the Western Hemisphere and throughout the Dollar Area, the Japanese empire in Manchuria, China and South East Asia, the German '*drang nach osten*' and occupation of Eastern and Central Europe, the Russian Empire stretching from the Baltic to the Pacific and south into Central Asia. Where these empires met and came into conflict, there has been war — in Eastern Europe, North Africa, the Middle East, in Southern and South East Asia. The Second World War broke up these spheres of influence in two ways: first, direct colonial rule was largely relaxed in the 1950s and 1960s, most erstwhile colonies achieved independence and some established socialist constitutions; secondly the spread of transnational companies has crossed the frontiers of earlier preserves. Nonetheless, in many areas neo-colonial influence still remains and a large sphere of influence in Eastern Europe was conceded to the USSR.

The current economic crisis is posing a major challenge to the political leaders of those powers which are large enough to be recognised by the giant transnational companies as important bases for their operations. This really means the USA, Japan, the European community under West German economic leadership, and in different ways the Soviet Union. The tendency to strengthen their defences and to keep others out of their spheres of influence is becoming more and more obvious, despite the hopeful words to the contrary which we quoted from Mr Gorbachev at the beginning. The USA is fastening its grip on the Caribbean and Latin America and in the Middle East. The European Community is developing the concept of "Fortress Europe" with close ties to Africa. Japan is extending its economic hold on South East Asia, but Japanese companies, with the largest world-wide investments of any country, have major economic interests also in Latin America, the USA itself and in Europe. In face of all these moves, the Soviet Union under Mr.Gorbachev's bold new leadership is developing its ties with Eastern Europe as part of the process of *perestroika*. Does all this mean once more the closing down of wider economic exchanges and a deepening depression?

Patterns of World Trade Today

There are two major gaps in the development of world trade today. The one everyone talks about is the $150 billion deficit in the trade balance of the USA with the rest of the world, mainly with Japan ($50 billions), developing countries $30 billions), the EEC ($25 billions) and Canada ($20 billions). But there are two even more intransigent deficits: those with the oil producing countries; these amount to $90 billions of which $40 billions is that of the developing countries and $30 billions that of developed industrial countries in Europe. The United States' deficit with the rest of the world has existed for a very long time, though it has not been nearly so big as today. It has been paid for in the past first by gold and then by Eurodollars. Today the gold has run out and the Eurodollars are no longer trusted, so that the United States is forced to borrow. If the USA were to cut back its trade deficit to reduce its borrowing and bring down interest rates, as some economists propose it should do, by the full $150 billions, that would reduce the whole of world trade by 8%. Prior to 1979 world trade was growing by 8% on average every year. Between 1979 and 1983 world trade hardly grew and since 1983 it averaged about 5%. So a cut of 8% would mean more than a whole year's growth lost with all the complications involved, especially those countries in the Third World least able to survive a loss.

The third great gap in world trade results from the collapse of the third world's share. Until 1983 the share of the Third World countries in world trade exchanges grew steadily and this was not only of the oil producers. Before that year the non oil producers had been able to overcome the effects of the oil price rise by increasing their borrowing. But after 1983 the sharp decline in their own commodity prices and the rising proportion of their exports committed to debt repayment began to reduce their capacity to import — from over 18% of world trade in 1983 to under 17% in 1986. It may be said that 17% or 18% of world trade is not a very large proportion. But the impact of the third world debt crisis has hardly yet been felt. If the United States were to cut back its foreign deficits by reducing imports but debt payments continued, many third world countries particularly in Latin America would no longer be able to pay.

As we have seen, a major gap in world trade is the failure of the oil exporting countries to import as much as they export, especially in trade with the developing countries which have no oil. The oil exporters run surpluses and the non-oil producing countries run deficits. This has been covered by borrowing through the commercial banking system. These debts are now causing acute concern in the banks that have lent the money. No more money is being lent and repayments are taking up a large proportion, often over half and even 100%, of the export earnings of developing countries. So their imports are being cut back and the whole growth of world trade is checked.

The answer is simple, even if its implementation is difficult. The industrial countries need to increase their imports from the non-oil producing developing countries and increase their exports to the oil producers. Then the oil producers could be compensated for their sales to the non oil producing developing countries. What is needed is to encourage a new triangle of trade, which would have the effect of raising the whole level of world trade exchanges. A simple diagram can serve as an illustration.

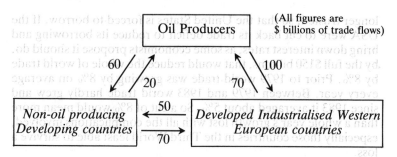

The flows here of nearly $400 billions amount to over a fifth of the total world trade. It is suggested that the initiative would have to come from the developed industrial countries in Europe, because it is unlikely that the USA or Japan would feel the need to join in such a project. If Europe were to act it would be better to include the whole of Europe, East and West.

If the Second World, as we may call the countries including the Soviet Union that are building socialism, were to take part in this joint action, then another 5% of the world's trade would be involved. This is about half of the socialist bloc's external trade. Nobody is expecting countries that are building socialism to come to the rescue of collapsing capitalism, unless it is very obviously in their interests to do so. The fact is that it may be. Firstly, the socialist states are themselves very heavily in debt to the capitalist bankers, and any action that raises the general level of world trade exchanges makes it easier for them, as it does for the developing countries, to sell their goods on the world market and repay their debts. Secondly, it is one of the aims of *perestroika* according to Professor Aganbegyan's book, *The Economics of Perestroika*, that the USSR should become an open economy. In the first instance, such openness will be limited to the other socialist states, but it is not intended to stop there. This is obviously recognised by Mr Gorbachev when he speaks of the relationship between disarmament and development.

A New Initiative to Expand World Trade.
What then would be the form of a joint initiative from first, second and third world countries to expand world trade and offset the danger of a major trade recession? The socialist countries have experience of various forms of long-term trade agreements, not only between each other but also with capitalist partners, both large companies and government organisations, in Finland, Austria and West Germany for example. Joint action could take place at a number of levels. Agreements between governments to expand

their trade exchanges in certain areas can make a start. But beneath this, there is the need for detailed agreements for expanded exchanges between regions, localities and enterprises. It is of major importance that one aspect of *perestroika* involves the ending of the Soviet Ministry of Foreign Trade's monopoly of all foreign trade. From now on not only separate ministries, but enterprises can enter into foreign trade agreements on their own initiative. What is essential is that external trade does not remain the victim of deflationary policies in the capitalist countries and of bureaucratic restrictions in the socialist countries, each country reducing its spending in order to reduce its imports and thus balancing trade exchanges at cumulatively lower levels, until one day some extraneous force: a specially good (or bad) harvest or a new invention, a mineral discovery or a cheaper way of producing something: starts off a virtuous circle of growth once more. The point to recognise is that international trade is not a zero-sum game, in which, if one country has more of it another must have less, but that it can be expanded by deliberate action, just as it can be contracted by default.

Trade exchanges are not simply a matter of reaching agreement among governments or between enterprises in general terms to promote an expansion in place of the current trend towards contraction. There have to be goods and services which each party wishes to sell or buy. There was always some truth in Ricardo's law of comparative advantage, that each country should concentrate its resources in producing what it is best able to produce. In this way all resources should be used to the best advantage.

The obvious drawback in the working of the law is that some countries would gain more advantage than others in the market, where some products bring higher rewards for the same application of labour and capital. This is because some products have substitutes, have less value added in their production, are more easily subject to increased productivity or are simply more easily cartelised so that monopoly prices can be charged. The countries most likely to suffer have always been in the Third World, where one cash crop or mineral was developed in each colony often at the expense of food production for local consumption. Diversification of trade has been the main aim of ex-colonial countries, particularly through the increase of local value-added by industrialisation. But this aim has often been rendered difficult to achieve by the protectionist measures of the industrial countries, by the operating policies of transnational companies and by higher levels of indebtedness incurred in the process of industrialisation.

The current problem of third world debt arises mainly from the declining levels of world trade and of the falling world prices of the products of third world countries. On average, primary commodity prices excluding oil, now stand at about three-quarters of the level they stood at in 1979-81. Oil prices are less than half what they were then. Much of the decline in trade follows directly from the protectionist measures activated especially by the industrialised countries often with strong support both from employers and employees' organisations in a period of high unemployment. The most protectionist measures of all are taken by the European Community against imports of food under the Common Agricultural Policy and these have their greatest impact on food producers in the third world countries. The results of deflationary policies by industrial countries in their home markets are in effect onslaughts on the exports of the third world countries.

Towards a Europe-Third World Conference.
Lower levels of international trade are also the result of inexperience in third world countries in developing new products which could be sold in the first world. Similar problems have arisen in the Second World of socialist countries where lack of attention to quality, packaging and to consumer preference has led to a concentration of trade on foodstuffs and raw materials. The point is made very forcibly by Professor Aganbegyan in his book. 60% of Soviet exports consists of electricity, fuels and raw materials. Only 20% consist of vehicles and machinery: while 20% of imports consist of foodstuffs, 35% of vehicles and machinery and another 15% of industrial consumer goods. As the Soviet Perestroika progresses, it is planned to increase the quality of goods and the responsiveness of producers to consumer demand, through direct connection of Soviet enterprises with the market, not only at home but also abroad. The USSR's huge reserves of fuels and raw materials will still provide a large part of the products for export, but the exchange of finished manufactures is to be greatly increased, so that foreign trade comes to make up a much larger proportion of the national income. Currently, exports account for no more than 10% of Soviet national income, compared with over 20% in the case of most industrial countries. The USSR plans to increase its international links first with the other planned economies in the Council for Mutual Economic Aid (CMEA) through long term trade agreements and joint ventures. To extend these links into the capitalist world would require development of some similar planning of trade to suit requirements.

A major criticism of such proposals in the past has been that the USSR and its CMEA allies simply had nothing to offer. They could barely feed themselves, economic growth was stagnant and the CMEA was no more than a dumping ground for goods which could not be sold at home. Now that Mr Gorbachev has confirmed all these criticisms and proposed structural reforms to overcome them, the time would seem to be ripe for a new initiative in international economic co-operation between East and West, not forgetting the South. All three worlds, First, Second and Third, are desperately in need of finding an alternative to a most damaging decline in world trade exchanges. World wide action is imperative if a deep recession is to be avoided. This involves some high level meetings — in the first instance of those governments which are actually concerned at the prospect of a major recession and believe that some joint action is required. At the regular meetings of the seven main capitalist powers the only proposals that are considered seem to be concerned with rates of interest and the exchange rates of their currencies, especially in relation to the dollar. Each government seems to believe that it is the responsibility of one of the others, not themselves, to take positive action to reflate their economy against any recessionary tendency. The obvious conclusion that they should agree to reflate on a common programme of positive action, with especial attention to the Third World is considered to be anathema.

In these circumstances it seems premature, even utopian, to call a World Economic Conference. Such conferences were singularly unproductive in the 1930s, despite the careful preparation for them of the League of Nations secretariat. Calling an all-European Conference might be more productive, if the aim was deliberately to expand trade exchanges not only across Europe, but between Europe and the Third World. The emphasis placed on Mr Gorbachev in his book on *Perestroika* on "a common European home" and which has been echoed by the foreign ministers of West Germany and Italy, suggests the need for practical activity to furnish the common home. What is called the "second basket" of the Helsinki process includes an expansion of trade exchanges, but it would be mistaken to make this an exclusive affair. The European Community of the western part of Europe is already exclusive enough. What Europe also has in common is a long history, much of it a regrettable history of close ties with what we now call the Third World much of which is a world of one-time European colonies. In the light of my earlier proposals for an expansion of triangular trade with the oil producing third world countries, it would be necessary to involve the oil producing states from the start.

In the last three years, 1985-87, crude oil prices have been as high as \$28 a barrel and as low as \$13.50. Prices appear currently to be steadying out at \$20. A low price for oil benefits especially the non-oil producing third world countries, particularly Brazil, India, Korea, Greece and Turkey and also the USA, Japan and Western Europe, where all except the UK and Norway are major oil importers. By contrast, it has serious implications for those third world oil exporters, chiefly Algeria, Indonesia, Mexico, Nigeria and Venezuela, which have large debts to repay, and also for the USSR which relies greatly on its oil/and gas exports and the UK which has a non-oil trade balance that is heavily in the red. Of course, the Middle East oil producers also suffer from a fall in oil prices, but their trade balances are influenced by the relative value of the dollar since oil prices are all quoted in dollars. The current situation of a low price for oil and a low value for the dollar is particularly troublesome, but only Iraq and Iran have any serious difficulty in balancing their foreign account. The middle eastern states have surpluses.

The oil price cannot, however be considered in isolation from other prices and, for the developing countries, especially the prices of other primary products. The non-oil producing countries have to pay for their oil and also repay their debts with their earnings from the sale of their own raw materials and foods. The level of interest rates is also important for them. Interest rates tend to fall as oil prices fall, since the United States has less need to borrow to pay for oil imports. It has been calculated by the World Bank that out of 15 major third world debtor countries the fall in the oil price in 1985-86, taking into account the effect on interest rates, caused a loss to the oil producers among the $24 billions, while the gain to the ten oil importers among them was only a little over 6 billions. A further fall, say to $10 a barrel, would certainly cause major defaults among the oil producing debtor countries and a serious banking crisis. What is more, any such fall in prices is likely to come as a result of a general decline in demand especially in the USA. The non-oil exporting third world countries will see the price of their products falling in line with oil prices. The conclusion must be that there would be gains all-round from policies designed to expand world demand, even if it involved some rise in the price of oil. It should not be difficult, therefore, to encourage oil producers as well as non-oil producers in the Third World to join in the proposed joint actions.

Detailed Proposals
This is not the place to go into any great detail about the forms which joint action for expanding world trade might take. There are already many different forms of counter trading, as it is now termed, in operations ranging from direct barter through several kinds of buy back agreement to multilateral compensation arrangements. International banks and other institutions have been highly innovative in creating solutions for problems facing countries and enterprises having large-scale requirements of raw materials and fuels or of productive plant, but no cash to pay for these until

income is generated by setting them to work. A problem arises of financing smaller projects which the bankers consider not to be worth their while to investigate. There are many alternative counter traders, but their services are often expensive and tied to particular suppliers which may not always prove to be appropriate. In cases of dire necessity the charity aid organisations have stepped in, but there is a general need of a special fund, such as is proposed by Mr Gorbachev, drawing, as he suggests, on voluntary, state and private contributions related to the reduction in military spending.

All the evidence obtained from the experience of arms conversion proposals suggests that these need to be of a most detailed sort, if they are to be acceptable to those whose jobs are likely to be lost by closing down military production, if they are to make use of the skills and productive capacity thereby released. Any conference that was to be envisaged to realise proposals for disarmament and development would need to generate a wide range of working groups on a particular economic sectors and areas of production. It is hoped that the Third World Trade and Technology Conference of non-governmental organisations from first, second and third world countires being held in Maputo at the end of May will help to indicate the direction in which such work could proceed. Projects on a vastly larger scale than anything that NGOs can achieve will be needed if the threat of world recession is to be countered and programmes for development firmly linked to agreement on disarmament.

One working group should be concerned with initiatives designed to reform the international economic order established in 1944 at Bretton Woods. It is not only necessary to criticise the very restrictive and even biased operations of the World Bank and International Monetary Fund and suggest reforms for these institutions, but also to go back to the original intentions of Keynes at Bretton Woods in at least two matters: the first is the need for a positively oriented International Trade Organisation to build the work of the General Agreement on Tariffs and Trade (GATT), so that a clearing house could be established to facilitate positive trade agreements instead of merely monitoring and encouraging reductions in negative obstacles to trade exchanges by tariffs and non-tariff weapons.

The second is the need to begin to move toward a world money. The USSR's moves towards a convertible rouble and the collapse of the dollar, taken together with the uncertain future of the European Community's money system, makes this a particularly opportune time to raise this question. The SDR (Special Deposit Reserve) already performs some of the functions of a world money in that it is a means of exchange in international transactions and a unit of account in setting prices. It is to some extent also a reserve (store of value) that can be drawn on by countries facing balance of payment problems. The total issue of SDRs, however, is still very small, rarely amounting to more than a tenth of the non-gold reserve holdings of any country. The importance of moving towards a world money which takes the place of any one nation's currency, is stressed by the evident lack of a currency that can replace the declining power of the dollar. Neither the yen nor the mark which represent the two main rivals to the United States are capable of replacing the dollar in view of the relatively limited military and economic power that lies behind these two otherwise remarkably successful currencies.

At the level of practical projects, working groups in particular fields of agriculture and industrial development will find in the pigeon holes of the specialised agencies of the United Nations, the Food and Agricultural Organisation, the World Health Organisation, the Children's Emergency Fund, the UN Development Programme and UNESCO, many projects which involve international trade and technology exchanges. Some of these are large schemes involving considerable resources: many will be quite small, but currently starved of funds for their progress. In addition, there are schemes for natural conservation and ecological protection, for example, in the protection of the rain forests, that require large-scale international cooperation. We have been warned by the ecologists that there is very little time left to take preventative action and that some action will require massive resources that could only be made available through reduction in military spending. Once again the experts know what needs to be done. Working groups of scientists and engineers could begin to allocate tasks and to commission further research work where it was needed. Is it really too much to hope that the threat of imminent world slump could just be enough to start a great new initiative in world development? It could be mankind's last chance.

4: Gorbachev's reforms:
A Great Opportunity

Dr Norbert Wieczorek

Since Secretary-General Gorbachev's article was published in *Pravda* last September, the number of people that believe that he is serious about his reform efforts has most definitely increased. At the same time, however, there has been an increase in the number of those doubting the ability or even willingness of the Soviet system to respond to these reform proposals.

If one views, from a distance, the massive problems associated with the reform of a system with an established bureaucratic structure including all of its ingrained privileges and shelters, one quickly realises the immensity of such an undertaking. In addition, the self-realisation and the pressure of the real world economic circumstances which have convinced the top leadership to act, must be translated into concrete action on all decision-making levels. This will be an arduous task not only because the USSR is an extremely large country with a correspondingly large population, but primarily because the individual Soviet citizen has no experience in the economic or social decision-making process, nor is there an example in Russian history which could serve as a guide. Along with the cultural and historical multiplicity of the Soviet Republics, which can lead to differing priorities and conflicts of interest, they have too little experience in articulating their interests freely and realistically. The doubter's view thus seems to be fairly realistic and possibly appealing to many.

In spite of all these potential obstacles, the charted course of reforms has a good chance of being realised. The reforms, interpreted in the classic Marxian sense, would allow the realignment of the modern production means and actual production. Assuming that — and there are definite signs to this effect — an attempt is being made to equally improve and develop many aspects of the Soviet Union, including a rise in the standard of living, then a degree of public support can be found, harnessed and, hopefully, organised in the population at large, although not necessarily in the western democratic sense.

It is critical that the leadership of the Soviet Union should be able to concentrate primarily on this domestic initiative. Thus the cold warriors of yesterday that continue, through constant calls for modernisation and arms build-up (most recently in conventional arms), to jeopardise the recent advances in arms reduction, should consider whether or not a successful outcome of the Soviet Union's necessary reforms and a redirecting of their human and material resources toward civil development would not be an even greater incentive to propel the arms reduction process forward.

Such a development would be to our own advantage because of the additional means that would be set free, which could then be used meaningfully in the fight against unemployment and poverty in our countries, and to alleviate the difficult state of many Third World nations. It is of the utmost importance, specifically in this regard, to sound out and exhaust all possibilities thoroughly.

One must realise, however, that the process in the Soviet Union could be enhanced from outside. The process can only be strengthened by us, if it becomes clear that Western countries are prepared to deal with parallel problems so that a potential threat would be alleviated. This could also serve as the basis for a meaningful and long term negotiated co-operation in the economic sphere, as well as scientific endeavour and cultural exchange between Western Europe and the Soviet Union and its allies.

The continued elimination of mutual threats, or potential threats, and the development of a security partnership can and will contribute to a bridging of the unnatural division of the economic and cultural entity of Western, Central, and Eastern Europe. Increased Western European co-operation and integration particularly in the European Community will facilitate this process and help to overcome existing political fears. A self-assured Europe, on the basis of two differing social systems could, without a doubt, be realistically conceivable.

In sum, although Gorbachev's proposals have yet to become concrete both in theoretical and practical forms, they offer a great opportunity. We must grasp the opportunity and realise the necessary adjustments on our part in order to render the reform in the Soviet Union a success. Our task is not to give advice or try to gain influence in the Soviet Union, but to say that we cannot make certain demands on the basis of our humanitarian and democratic principles is untrue. Nor must we give up our optimism for a closer economic and cultural co-operation. However, it is vital that the demands and suggestions that we feel obliged to make, we must apply to our own society no less critically.

5: Taking Gorbachev Seriously

Maarten van Traa, Bob de Ruiter

The signing of the International Nuclear Forces-treaty has caused a widespread optimism about world affairs. Many hopes have been expressed that it is a turning point to a better era, in which international co-operation and disarmament will be promoted. This is not only the expectation of large segments of public opinion. This is also the view of the two world leaders, Ronald Reagan and Mikhail Gorbachev. They have declared on several occasions that further progress in the field of East-West relations can be made. I share this optimism, but to a certain degree.

Glasnost
The reading of Soviet newspapers has become much more interesting with the new wind of change in the USSR. Since Gorbachev is the first among equals, it is admitted that the Soviet-society has to cope with severe problems and that life in the USSR is not always easy. Gorbachev urges for fundamental changes and emphasizes the importance of 'glasnost' and 'perestroika'. Although it is too early to predict the outcome, there is no question that he has set a promising development in motion.

It is clear that Gorbachev's statements on disarmament and arms control are not only of symbolic value. He is in a large part responsible for the making of the INF-treaty, since it only became a reality after some substantial concessions from his side. Gorbachev was willing to conclude the treaty on intermediate nuclear forces although it did not provide for limitations on the French and British nuclear arsenals (which are being modernised). Moreover, the treaty did provide for the elimination of the so-called short range intermediate forces (SRINF), a category of weapons in which the Soviet Union had a superiority in numbers. Gorbachev could have insisted that these weapons were not under consideration — they were not even mentioned in the original zero-option which was proposed by NATO in 1981. But he didn't.

So Gorbachev must be taken seriously. And thanks to the campaign for openness, the articles in the *Pravda* are much more interesting than in the past, especially when they are written — or at least signed — by the secretary general himself. But also in the age of 'new thinking' the temptation to use rhetoric can apparently not always be resisted.

Comprehensive security
Gorbachev promotes the idea of the establishment of a so-called "comprehensive system of international security". This idea has been advanced by the 27th CPSU Congress two years ago. Since then, it has won backing from many countries, mostly the allies of the Soviet Union. In the Western world, to use the words of the party-leader, "many influential forces continue adhering to outdated conceptions concerning ways for ensuring national security". According to Gorbachev, the proposed system could function on the basis of the UN Charter and within the framework of the United Nations. "Its ability to function will be ensured by the strict observance of the Charter's demands, additional unilateral obligations of states as well as confidence measures and international co-operation in all spheres". This system could become a reality, he adds, "only if all means of mass annihilation were destroyed". In this context, Gorbachev points also to the relationship between disarmament and development, confirmed at the September '87 UN-Conference in New York. The importance of a co-ordinated approach, aimed at development of the Third World, is underlined. A world in which "huge masses of people are suffering from almost permanent malnutrition is not a safe world".

Questions
These proposals sound good. We, too adhere to the concept of a non-nuclear world. Non-violent means of conflict resolution ought to govern inter-state relations. that is to say: conflict-resolution should be regulated without the use or the pressure of military means. And of course, the vital importance of development of the third world countries cannot be emphasized to often in an era in which, as Gorbachev says, a continent like Africa can find itself on the brink of death from starvation.

But the question remains: how do we achieve these ends? The answers to this question in Gorbachev's article are not very convincing. In fact, the article is markedly utopian or rather propagandistic in several aspects. The attention is concentrated on the goals to be achieved, not on the way to reach them. Consequently, the proposed means are not very realistic. Simple solutions do not exist. We would like to discuss some of the so-called "bricks" from which, according to Gorbachev, one can start building the future system of security.

The conventional forces

One of the urgent problems to be solved in order to achieve the goal of a nuclear-free Europe is the apparent imbalance in conventional forces of NATO and Warsaw pact in the latter's favour. The political party we represent, admits that together with the removal of the last nuclear weapon systems from Europe, a conventional balance, preferably on the lowest possible level, must be established. The reason is that the process of denuclearisation must not increase the risk of a conventional war, because such a war, too, would be devastating. Gorbachev proposes: "If an imbalance, disproportion exist, let us remove them. We do not tire saying this all the time". Although it is of crucial importance that the Soviet Union recently acknowledged that there is, indeed, an imbalance, it is misleading to suggest that it can be removed immediately. The MBFR negotiations started in Vienna in 1973 and in the years that followed, Moscow showed no eagerness to remove imbalances. Although it is recently reported that some progress has been made, when Gorbachev writes in this context that the Soviet Union is a pioneer, he must be more specific. And when he urges for an accord on a 'defence strategy' and 'military sufficiency', he ought to deal with this question too: what should a defensive and non-provocative conventional defence look like?

Defence spending

Gorbachev raises the question of the comparability of defence spending. "I think that given proper effort already within the next two or three years we will be able to compare the figures that are of interest to us and our partners and which could symmetrically reflect the expenditures of the two sides". The message reads that such a procedure can be of use to efforts aimed at disarmament and arms control. Besides the fact that in theory such an agreement does not forestall the possibility of a mutual balanced rise in expenditures, we doubt that procedures of this kind can be of any use. After all, we are not dealing with administrative or technical problems, but with a political one. If a government is convinced that it is obliged to raise military expenditures in order to achieve certain political ends — be it "the preservation of peace", the "glory of the nation" or the protection of "vital interests" abroad — then it will try to spend the money.

Nuclear Weapons and foreign policy

Here we touch on the more fundamental aspects, which are

nevertheless neglected in Gorbachev's contribution. Conventional and nuclear weapons serve political purposes. It's not only the 'military industrial complex' that has a direct interest in defence spending, that can be blamed for the ever raising expenditures. International-political ends are also at stake.

You don't have to be a Marxist-Leninist to note that, for example, the United States has "vital interests" in the Third World and that repeatedly these interests were defended by military means. The conventional forces were called upon to realise several military interventions in third world countries. The nuclear forces, on the other hand, were used as a kind of general support of third world policies, in particular outside the 'recognised' spheres of influence. In a vast number of international crises the nuclear threat was made visible in order to intimidate the opponents, most notably the Soviet Union and/or her regional allies (for instance the Korea- and Cuba-crises, the Middle East-crises in '56, '78 and '73).

Although in public declarations the security aspects prevailed, the 'real' economic interests were of importance too. The rise in military expenditures during the Reagan administration must also be understood against the background of assumed "global responsibilities".

Casper Weinberger made this very clear when he spoke about the "nation's fundamental vital interests and the foreign policy needed to protect them". According to Weinberger, it was an imperative "to protect access to foreign markets and overseas resources in order to maintain the strength of the United States' industrial, agricultural and technological base and the nation's economic well-being".

Of course, the availability of impressive conventional and nuclear forces is also of crucial importance for the Soviet Union. Her superpower-status depends heavily on it and the intention of the Soviet leadership to maintain this status, by military means if necessary, was demonstrated repeatedly. Is Gorbachev ready to give it up?

He writes: "Unconditional observance of the United Nations Charter and the right of people's sovereignty to choose the roads and forms of their development, revolutionary or evolutionary, is an imperative condition of universal security". Does this statement mean that the Soviet Union is prepared to abstain from "the right" to intervene with military means in socialist countries, when — as has been said in connection with the Czechoslovakian events in August 1968 — "policies are pursued that can threaten the common interests of the socialist community". And does it mean, that the Soviet Union is prepared to retreat out of Afghanistan, so that the people there can choose their own 'evolutionary' or even 'reactionary' forms of development? Gorbachev's statements would be more convincing if he could give an answer on questions of this kind.

By the way, we do not argue the "usefulness" of armaments in order to discourage attempts to disarm. On the contrary, we would like to emphasize the importance of such attempts. But if we are to succeed in the long run, we must be aware of the way armaments have been used until today.

Disarmament and development

We already suggested, that it can be misleading to assume a harmony of (international) interests. In many views on the relationship between disarmament and development this harmony is nevertheless supposed. It is believed that any progress towards any of these objectives, will constitute progress for both. We will not discuss all the aspects of the relationship, but we would like to emphasize this: economic development of third world countries can be also a source of conflict with western countries, whose interests are — to say the least — not always served by such a development. Therefore, it can stimulate arms procurement in the western world.

Today, the minority of the world population which lives in the rich world, consumes most of the scarce resources. This disequilibrium would inevitably be affected if a development process in the Third World gained momentum: it would not make the rich world still richer, at least not in the short run. The advocates of a New International Economic Order ought to realise that. As Gunner Myrdal stated: "The blind truth is that without radical changes in the consumption patterns in the rich countries, any pious talk about a new economic order is humbug".

Gorbachev, too, tends to neglect the conflicting interests. Although he admits that the "economic interests of individual countries or their groups are so different and contradictory", he ignores these differences when he speaks about "the imperatives of the time that compel us to institutionalise common sense notions". He states: "It was not philanthropy which prompted our proposal to agree on the reduction of interest payments under bank credits and the elaboration of extra benefits for the least developed nations. This holds benefits for all, namely a secure world".

Indeed, this proposal was not prompted by philanthropy, because Gorbachev will be aware of the fact that these interest payments are sent to Western capitals, not to Moscow. And it is undeniable that, besides "the benefits of a secure future", such a kind of arrangement will hold losses for the Western world.

To avoid any misunderstanding: We are much in favour of a generous settlement of the debts-crisis. It's a shame that, for example, the annual interest payments of many of the poorest countries exceed largely the offered aid-funds or their exports. We do also support the proposal to diminish military expenditures and to use these extra funds for development aid. But if one wants an alleviation of the debt-burden, and, more in general, a programme for disarmament and development, it does not suffice to emphasize that "this holds benefits for all".

Conclusion

Although it is not worked out yet, Gorbachev's prospect of a "comprehensive security system" remains attractive. The need for fundamental changes is not questioned.

Enhancing the role of the United Nations in solving international conflicts, is an urgent task but it is difficult to accomplish. Until today, the authority of the UN has been challenged over and over again. The efforts for instance of the UN Secretary-General Perez de Quellar to conclude an armistice in the Iran-Iraq war have been unsuccessful. And the resolutions of the Security Council did not have any significant impact. It is apparently easy for countries to pay lip-service to the goals of the United Nations as long as their own policies are not called into question. In general: whenever perceived vital interests are at stake, states are not willing to subordinate national policies to UN policies. Will the Soviet Union be prepared to transmit far-reaching authorities to the United Nations for the sake of peace and the general well-being, as suggested by Gorbachev? That remains to be seen. He will surely not be prepared to make an unconditional surrender to the UN (and neither is the western world). So it would have been more interesting if Gorbachev had spelled out the conditions under which he would be ready to accept an enhanced role for the Security Council of the UN. His rather vague declarations need to be elaborated to be really attractive. Moreover, he tends to overlook the existence of conflicting interests. The dichotomy between the doctine of peaceful coexistence, which means also political struggles, and a general conflict-free approach seems to us rather large. And after all, the immediate goal is not a world without conflicts, but a world in which conflicts can be resolved by non-violent means. Thus, ignoring conflicts will not bring us any further.

Finally, we would like to recall that attention must never be concentrated almost exclusively on the end. The reality itself must be studied as well in order to develop an appropriate strategy to change it. In the past many attempts to create a safer world have failed, because of a lack of realism. The American president Wilson believed in his League of Nations. Subsequently, critical analyses were branded as being unhelpful. "If it won't work, it must be made to work", he said once. But Wilson's system didn't work.

Gorbachev's "comprehensive security system" deserves a critical analysis too. And of course: such a system cannot be established at once. It can only be the outcome of long term policies of detente, arms control, and the elaboration of a new North-South strategy, with the participation of the Soviet Union. But closer co-operation, also in the framework of the UN and other multilateral bodies, can be of great importance to make conflict resolution a more peaceful business. In that sense Gorbachev's article has to be welcomed.

6: Warfare or Welfare

Keith and Anne Buchanan

"The warfare state militates against a global welfare state." In this terse statement the Russell Foundation's Development and Disarmament Initiative* summarises the tragic and overriding reality of world society as humanity approaches the last decade of the century. The world in which we live, the world we have allowed our leaders to structure for us, is one in which militarism is, in Ruth Leger Sivard's words, "creating an atmosphere in which distrust and animosity grow and the cooperative endeavour necessary to mutual security and all progress diminishes."

The DDI — and the recent initiatives of Mikhail Gorbachev — are an attempt to confront this deadly linkage. They offer us, poised on the brink of global collapse, existing from day-to-day in the shadow of a terminal nuclear conflict, possibly the last opportunity to draw back from the abyss and to pool our energies in creating together a world fit for humankind to live in. For their common theme is that peace and justice are inseparable; that the motive for militarism is the protection of the "right" of a rich minority to a disproportionate share of the world's i.e. other people's resources; and that we have to accept — and implement — St Ambrose's belief that "the World is given to all and not only to the rich" if we would rid ourselves of the militarism which lies, like some suffocating incubus, over all humanity. . . And that if we fail in this there can be no end to that insensate destruction of the natural world which menaces rich and poor alike.

It is an immense and uplifting opportunity we are offered — and just what is at stake may become clearer if we look at the ongoing and cumulative costs to humanity, the physical cost and the psychological costs, of putting into place today's weapon systems, *even if not used. . .*

A Gradual Brutalization
One of the major casualties of the arms race is the human spirit, for

*See above page 21.

in the long and desperate struggle against the ever-present threat to the continued survival of mankind we have continually to put at risk our own humanity. For we can, most of us, preserve our sanity only by anaesthetizing ourselves against the unthinkable and unbearable menace posed to our day-to-day existence by the ongoing arms race, anaesthetizing ourselves against the deafening slogan-mongering of a sensation-hungry and profit-motivated media apparatus. Yet in so doing we are in danger of losing that sense of compassion and that capacity for indignation at the arrogant and insolent treatment of the great majority of our fellow-beings by those of our leaders whose power-drunk policies we are opposing.

Human solidarity is threatened, and this threat is further enhanced by those who see in the exploitation of fear and the accentuation of distrust between peoples an opportunity for windfall profits. It is a telling comment on the extent to which this neurosis has progressed in the USA — and on the type of opportunists this sickness has spawned — that the sale of war toys has increased 600% since 1982 to a total value of over $1 billion in 1985 (which exceeds the GNP of some ten African states). And this association of war with fun and sport from an early age desensitizes and brutalizes; these trends are magnified by a spate of films such as *Rambo*, *Red Dawn* or *Invasion USA* which create a dehumanized perception of the Other (i.e. the Russians) and thus yet further accentuate the initial fear and distrust. . . An obsession with violence which is further catered for among adults by various types of "war games", survivalist camps providing military training and mercenary training schools.

Victims of Nuclear Madness
Many have already become direct victims as the result of the testing of nuclear weapons. The most obvious groups here are the Japanese and the indigenous peoples of the Pacific, the nuclear testing ground for French and American nuclear programmes. They include the groups deliberately exposed by the US military, all whose basis for daily life, the resources of the sea, has been poisoned by radioactive fallout and all those who have suffered the genetic consequences of radiation. These latter include also the Australian Aboriginals who were exposed to Britain's bomb tests and the troops of all those nations involved in atomic weapons testing. And to these victims of nuclear madness must be added all these who have suffered genetic damage or death in the process of uranium mining and as a result of the operation or malfunctioning of nuclear power plants whose existence is largely due to their production in the nuclear process of weapons-grade fissile substances.

Rosalie Bertell comments: "The global victims of the radiation pollution related to nuclear weapon production, testing, use and waste conservatively number 13 million. The current rate of weapon production globally (1985) generates between 7,000 and 15,000 victims yearly ... even without further nuclear weapon testing."

The Unseen Victims

The increasing militarization of global society which is one result of the Cold War "stand-off" involves an accelerating drain on world resources. Those resources, whether of raw materials, skilled labour, or capital, are swallowed up by the weapons race, which in turn is based on an industrial machine whose robotization makes many workers superfluous. The extreme example is provided by the war machine of the United States whose expansion is largely fuelled by extraction of resources from the uttermost ends of the earth. The financial costs of this manic programme are met by extortion from the poorer sectors of society and by the sucking in of capital from developed and developing nations alike. One of the aims of the programme was to bring about the collapse of the Soviet system as it endeavours to keep up in the competition; a more likely result is global financial chaos as US indebtedness piles up, and the collapse of an increasing number of nations as their economies are drained of the resources needed for development.

There has long been a ghastly symmetry between the spiralling superprofits of that favoured constellation of military contractors which enjoys a symbolic relationship with the US government and the spiralling waste of human lives in the countries of the periphery. And under conditions of a booming, automatized, war economy the old, the poor, the sick and the jobless of the countries of the centre are as expendable as — though more visible than — those who live so briefly and desperately in the forests and backlands of the periphery. The consequences have been somberly outlined by Rajni Kothari: "even if a nuclear war does not take place but only the preparations for it, these alone, along with other trends of the present capitalist economy, can still lead to the death of 250 to 300 million people — the expected casualty level of a nuclear war."

The Corruption of Science

In these "preparations" a essential role is being played by the scientific community. Kothari speaks of a global project "the aim of which is to put an end to humanity and civilization (and which) may be a success even without a holocaust." Our minds recoil from such a thesis as surely an exaggeration. Yet such a reaction is in large measure conditioned by a desperate belief in the integrity, even the benevolence, of the scientific community. Certainly, some scientists have distinguished themselves by their long and active campaign against the eagerness with which their colleagues have allowed themselves to be degraded into "call-boys" of the military-industrial-scientific establishment. But as Kothari reminds us, "hundreds of thousands of scientists" *are* involved in a global project, "the aim of which is to put an end to humanity and civilization." Sir Martin Ryle, towards the end of a distinguished scientific life, commented "Sadly, some 40% of professional engineers and probably more physicists in the UK are engaged in devising new ways of killing people; the US figures are I think much the same." We may blame Government, he points out, for the distortions of the distribution of expenditure and also powerful commercial pressures but, he observed, "Sadly that is not the whole story." The lure of challenging problems and unlimited funds exercises powerful seduction on young scientists and the old belief that "besides his own narrow field of research ... the scientist has a particular social responsibility in being aware of what is going on — and saying when he feels it to be wrong" is no longer a guiding principle.

The science which now menaces us all is, it must be recalled, part of a military-*industrial*-scientific establishment. This means that it becomes inevitably dominated by the same force which dominates western industrial society as whole; in other words, by the profit motive. Science is only marginally concerned with human needs, for the satisfaction of these has a low priority to most industrialists or to the governments whose funds play an increasing role in shaping industrial policy and research. And the military in the complex, which is today's largest single consumer of government derived funds, is, also by definition, concerned less with human welfare than illfare. . . .

"Saving the presence of life on earth..."

For us, as for probably good many other readers, one of the most hopeful — and the most novel — feature of Mikhail Gorbachev's recent initiatives lies in the way in which they break out of the sterile and dated mould into which the American-Soviet exchanges on disarmament had tended to become congealed. These exchanges have been dominantly concerned with the narrow issues of disarmament seen in a purely military sense, with continual emphasis on concepts such as "parity" between the two major world powers, on parity in nuclear weapons and the various kinds of disparity which might follow any reduction or elimination of nuclear arms. Such exchanges involved a narrow concept of the term peace and involved also the relegation of most of humanity to the role of mere spectators in what was for them, no less than for the two main protagonists in the exchanges, a matter of life and death. The Gorbachev initiatives invite us to take a much wider vision of the concept of worldpeace. They remind us that such a peace involves not merely a real and lasting agreement on nuclear issues between the USA and the USSR but also the termination of the chronic militarization of global society and of those ongoing "regional wars" which make a travesty of the concept of peace for untold millions of our fellows, whose lives and hopes and sufferings have somehow become irrelevant. But ultimately, peace rests upon justice, for there can be no peace in a world in which the weak and poor are plundered by the strong and rich to maintain a grossly unbalanced use of resources: indeed, as we have seen, the function of most militarism is the maintenance of this injustice, this "freedom to plunder."

The initiatives are a major step towards translating into practical politics a "new philosophic vision of the world." They recognise clearly that the basic issue is less a military and technological one than a political and psychological one so that an essential core of the problem is the "trust of the states and peoples in one another."

This process of confidence-building is seen as proceeding at two levels — the level of the individual and the international level. What is involved is nothing less than the arresting of that ongoing brutalization of humanity, that "militarization of the mind": to use Gorbachev's phrase, of which some examples were given earlier. Here, the initiatives propose that the UN should play a major role by working out a world information programme designed not only to familiarize peoples with one another's lives but above all, aimed at "ridding the flow of information of the 'enemy image' stereotypes." It is crucial, we feel, to break the Western media's monopoly on how most people see the world.

At the state level, too, it is contemplated that the UN would play a vital role. There is a realistic emphasis on building upon those small but important beginnings of the long process of arresting the headlong race to destruction and the models cited — the inspection by a group of US Congressmen of the controversial radar facilities at Krasnoyarsk, the installation and adjustment of their instruments by US scientists in the area of the Soviet nuclear testing range — represent critically important first steps in this process. The voluntary Soviet moratorium on testing, the unequivocal commitment to "no first use" and to the goal of the elimination of all nuclear weapons, represent major attempts to put into place yet further building blocks of trust between states. These actions have to be seen, not as some sort of proof that deterrence works, as many Western politicians and the Western media have claimed but as manifestations of an attempt to implement the vision behind Mikhail Gorbachev's initiatives, as illustrations of a dedicated struggle, against tremendous odds, to "preserve human civilisation." And in this struggle, it is emphasised, all the Soviet proposals are open to negotiation and the various concrete measures would be supervised by a stronger United Nations.

Rebuilding the Structure of International Order and Cooperation.

This emphasis on the United Nations is especially to be welcomed, coming as it does at a time when the UN and its agencies are being subjected to ever-increasing and intentionally destructive pressures. This weakening of the UN, and the failure to implement various UN resolutions, has struck at the whole basis of world order and the global trend toward the "law of the jungle" is further accentuated by the flouting of decisions of the International Court of Justice.

The initiatives propose a series of steps by which these processes could be reversed and which are designed to restore the UN to its original role as the world's major security body. They not only reassert the importance of the unconditional observance by all nations of the UN Charter and see the proposed security plan as functioning within the framework of the UN; they see the UN as having a major role in continually monitoring the military situation and averting — or limiting — any armed conflict; they propose wider use of UN military observers and UN peace-keeping forces; even more interestingly they see that the whole issue of the relationship between disarmament and development should be a major concern of the UN and that the problems of ecological security which menace this fragile earth should be tackled by international cooperation within the framework of the UN Special Programme.

Such proposals represent important additional "building blocks" in the arduous task of restoring faith and trust between peoples. The cement in this process of rebuilding would be found in the collaboration of the people of all nations in tackling the problems of feeding, housing, educating and keeping healthy all the world's population. The resources of capital and skilled labour which a cessation of the arms race would make available provide the basis for creating, at long last, a world fit for human beings to live in. And, not least, as an American participant at the International Forum 'For a Nuclear-Free World, for the Survival of Humanity' pointed out, such positive collaboration can "help reverse the trend towards science being captured for military purposes."

But for us the outstanding feature of Mikhail Gorbachev's

initiatives is his insistence that the survival of humanity is too important an issue to be left to politicians alone, that it is for the peoples of the world themselves to insist, through their governments and non-governmental organisations; that the time has come for them to assert their right — and the right of their children — to life, in a world without war. And, coupled with this, his dedicated courage taking the critical first steps which may make it possible for this vision to become reality.

References

Hannes Alfvén, "Annihilators and Omnicide" in *Development Dialogue*, Dag Hammarskjöld Foundation, Uppsala, 1984: 1-2.

Center for Defense Information, *The Defense Monitor*, Washington DC, especially: XV/2, 1986, "Militarism in America"; XVI/1 , 1987, "The Unravelling of Nuclear Arms Treaties" ; XVI/2, 1987, "Soviet Compliance with Arms Agreements".

Mikhail Gorbachev, *Realities and Guarantees for a Secure World*, Moscow, 1987.

International Forum "For a Nuclear-Free World, for the survival of Humanity", *The Meeting in the Kremlin*, Moscow, 1987.

Rajni Kothari, "Communications for Alternative Development" in *Development Dialogue* 1984: 1-2.

Martin Ryle's Letters, edited by M Rowan-Robinson, London, 1985.

Juan Somavía, "The Transitional Power Structure & International Information in *Development Dialogue*, 1981: 2 (the whole issue is on a, 'New World Information and Communication Order').

7: Recovering Research and Science

Marek Thee

1. Promises and threats of science and technology

Science-based modern technology is today a cardinal variable of human development. It is the mainspring and motor force of economic performance, productivity and the progress of civilisation. At the same time, however, science-based modern technology is also cause for concern. We are becoming increasingly alarmed by environmental degradation, pollution, depletion of primary resources, alienation, genetic engineering and, above all, by the militarisation of technology. Clearly, science and technology exert a pervasive impact on contemporary society, on our culture and way of life — for good and evil. On the quantitative and qualitative input of science and technology into our endeavours depend the nature, dynamics and level of human progress. Any attempt to comprehend better the world around us, our national and international predicaments, including problems of peace and war, must take into account the symbiotic workings of science and technology. This includes their institutional setup, their structure, drive and mode of operation.

In this paper I would like to draw attention to the impact of science and technology on two interrelated issues: of disarmament and development.

2. Disparities in the North-South distribution of R&D

It is laboratory research and development (R&D) that effectuates the application of science and technology on our economy and environment, on education and health and on buttressing our security. R&D is a huge establishment employing millions of scientists and engineers spread all over the globe, with an annual budget of thousands of millions of dollars.

In a concise definition of R&D, UNESCO notes that it comprises

> any creative systematic activity undertaken in order to increase the stock of knowledge, to devise new applications. It includes

fundamental research (i.e., experimental or theoretical work undertaken with no immediate practical purpose in mind), applied research in such fields as agriculture, medicine, industrial chemistry, etc., (i.e. research directed primarily towards a special practical aim or objective), and experimental development work leading to new devices, products or processes.[1]

Being a vital and socio-economically sensitive activity, the workings of R&D are largely screened from the public eye. Precise data of R&D are sparse, shrouded in confidentiality and secrecy, for both industrial-commercial and security reasons. The problem is amplified by the interpenetration of civilian and military R&D. where the latter has captured a key position in all R&D (see below). Some idea of the size, costs and North-South disparities in the global distribution of R&D is provided by UNESCO's data collection on employment and expenditure on R&D. Below are four tables of aggregate data on the basis of UNESCO statistics.

Table 1
Estimated number of scientists and engineers engaged in R&D, 1970 and 1980

		estimated number	*estimated number per million population*
World total	1970	2,608,100	708
	1980	3,756,100	843
Developed countries	1970	2,401,600	2,238
	1980	3,359,102	2,875
Developing countries	1970	206,500	79
	1980	396,998	121

Source: *UNESCO Statistical Yearbook 1985*, Table 5.1.

Table 2
Estimated expenditure for R&D for 1970 and 1980

		estimated amount (millions of US$)	*as % of GNP*
World total	1970	62,101	2.04
	1980	207,801	1.78
Developed countries	1970	60,677	2.36
	1980	195,377	2.24
Developing countries	1970	1,424	0.30
	1980	12,424	0.43

Source: *UNESCO Statistical Yearbook 1985*, Table 5.2.

Table 3
Estimated number of scientists and engineers in research and development (R&D), 1980

	Population (in thousands)	as % of total	Number engaged in R&D	as % of total	Number per million population
World total	4,453,000		3,756,100		843
Developed countries	1,168,000	26.0	3,359,102	89.4	2,875
Developing countries	3,285,000	74.0	396,998	10.6	121

Table 4
Estimated R&D expenditures, 1980

	GNP (billion US$)	GNP per capita US$	R&D expenditure (million US$)	as % of total	as % of GNP	R&D expenditure per each S&E (US$)
World total	11,666	2,619	207,801			55,324
Developed countries	8,958	8,477	195,377	94.0	2.24	58,163
Developing countries	2,708	794	12,424	6.0	0.43	31,295

Source (Table 3 & 4): *UNESCO Statistical Yearbook 1985*, Tables 1.1, 5.1, 5.2; Ruth Leger Sivard, *World Military and Social Expenditures 1983*.

Although some details may be questionable,[2] as a whole the data in the above tables are revealing indeed.

The most recent comparative data available derive from 1980. However, the trends and dynamics into the 1980s are plain. There has been a steep rise in the global number of scientists and engineers (S&E) engaged in R&D. From 1970 to 1980 this increase amounted to 44 per cent. At the same time, world expenditures on R&D multiplied 3.35 times in current dollars and 2.5 times above the rate of inflation. This indicates an accelerated progression in capital-intensive R&D.

At the same time, cumulatively there was an increase in the gap between the level of R&D in developed and in developing countries. Taken in isolation, the percentage growth of both S&E engaged in R&D, and of R&D expenditures was higher in developing than in developed countries; in absolute figures the disparites have been augmenting forcefully. The developing countries comprise 74 per cent of the world's population; they increased the number of S&E engaged in R&D by 190,498 and their expenditure on R&D by US $11 billion. This obviously relates mainly to a limited number of more advanced developing countries.

Figure 1
Number of scientists & engineers, 1970-1980

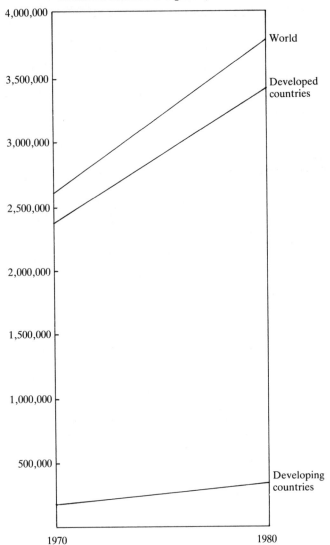

Source: Table 1.

Figure 2
R&D expenditure (in million US$) 1970-1980

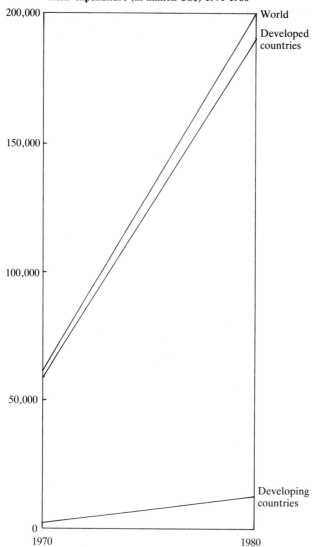

Source: Table 2.

Figure 3
Percentage share of scientists & engineers, 1980

100%
89.4%
10.6%
a
b
c
a — world
b — developed countries
c — developing countries

Figure 4
Percentage share of R&D expenditures, 1980

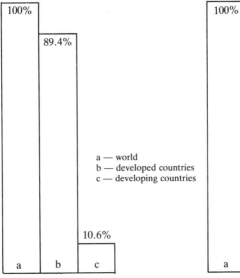

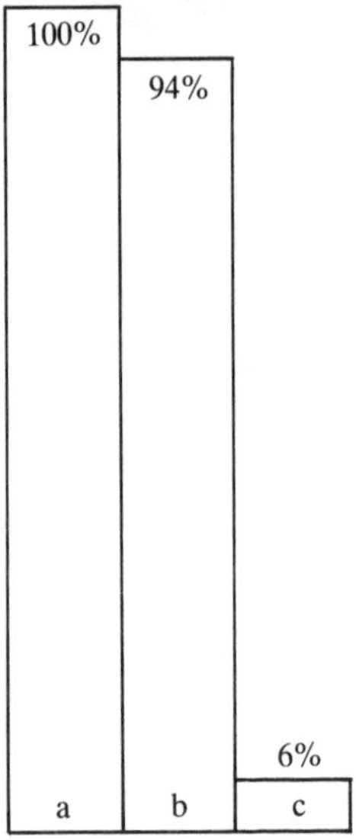

100%
94%
6%
a
b
c

Figure 5
Number of scientists & engineers per million of population, 1980

2,857
843
121
a
b
c
a — world
b — developed countries
c — developing countries

Figure 6
R&D expenditures per each scientist & engineer, 1980 (US dollars)

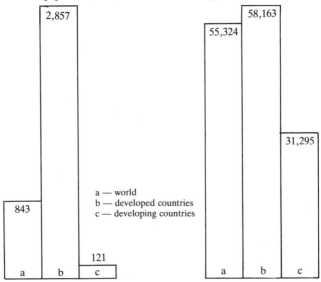

58,163
55,324
31,295
a
b
c

Source: Tables 3 & 4.

Simultaneously, the developed countries, with 26 per cent of the world's population, expanded R&D manpower by 957,502 S&E, five times as much as in developing countries; and R&D expenditure by nearly 135 billion US dollars, over 12 times as much as in developing countries. In 1980 the share of developing countries in global R&D — without taking into account the disproportion in the number of population and the economic differentiation within the developing countries themselves — remained at 10.6 per cent in S&E manpower and at 6 per cent in R&D expenditure. The number of S&E engaged in R&D per million population remained nearly 24 times higher in developed than in developing countries.

The more we delve into details, the gloomier the picture becomes. Thus, for instance, for Africa (with a population of 476 million in 1980), the percentage of world S&E engaged in R&D in 1980 was only 0.4 per cent and of global R&D expenditure 0.3 per cent; the respective figures for Latin America and the Caribbean (with a population of 362 million in 1980) were 2.4 per cent of global S&E engaged in R&D and 1.8 per cent of world expenditure on R&D. There were only 86 S&E engaged in R&D per million population in Africa, and 251 in Latin America and the Caribbean, compared to 2,875 in developed countries.[3]

An important drawback in the new R&D dynamics, as far as the developing countries are concerned, is the propensity towards capital-intensive activity. Per head of S&E, developed countries spent in 1980 twice as much in financial resources as developing countries. With a GNP per capita 10.6 times higher than in developing countries spent 2.24 per cent of their GNP on R&D, whereas developing countries could only afford 0.43 per cent of their GNP.

The above data bring into relief the widening North/South gap in R&D activity. In view of the critical overall importance of R&D for economic performance and socio-economic growth, this evolution underlines also the growing economic disparities between the developed and the developing world.

3. Militarisation of R&D

A critical factor in the skewed distribution of R&D between developed and developing countries is the militarisation of R&D, and the weight of military-orientated R&D in the totality of R&D activity. This has dire consequences for economic development, both within the major powers involved in the arms race and in developing countries. Moreover the thrust of military R&D is a major driving force behind the arms race which circumscribes both the rich and the poor nations. The militarisation of R&D not only affects human well-being and economic progress North and South, but is also crucial in shaping the horizons of war and peace. The working of military R&D has become a common denominator for the intensity of the arms race and economic decay.

By "military R&D" we subsume mission-orientated R&D activity comprising basic and applied research, including development, testing and experimental production of new weapons and weapon systems. It further includes the improvement and modernisation of existing weapons and weapon systems.

Military R&D was instrumental to starting modern large-scale science-based R&D, and thus set the course of its development. The meeting and fusion of science and technology evolved in a long historical process through the stages of the Industrial Revolution, culminating in the emergence of the nuclear age and the explosion of modern military technology. The real birthplace of contemporary R&D was the World War II Manhatten Project. This was the first large-scale laboratory effort, employing some 150,000 trained scientific and technical staff, to link closely basic and applied research, and with astounding results: atomic weapons saw the light of the day. This success animated massive coordinated R&D, and gave military R&D, conceived as an extraordinary force multiplier, a lead in this domain. Coinciding with war effort lingering on from World War II into the Cold War, military R&D profited from a climate in which major powers were eager to invest in large undertakings which might promise decisive, even ultimate, strength in the contest for world dominance.

3.1 Order of magnitude

No exact data on the size and dimensions of global military R&D are available. Secrecy is here practised to the extreme, far more than in civilian R&D. A few Western countries do publish some figures, but their accuracy is uncertain and may not disclose the full range of involvement. Different aspects of military R&D are concealed in diverse budgetary expenditures: in the case of the United States, for instance, nuclear-weapon R&D in the books of the Energy Department, while military space exploration in the budget of the National Aeronautics and Space Adminstration (NASA). The Soviet Union does not publish any data on its massive military R&D,[4] nor does China, another of the six major powers engaged in military R&D.

However, some useful indicators on the order of magnitude of world military R&D can be found in existing scholarly computations on world manpower and expenditure on military R&D.

Let us start on general estimates of the share of the global R&D

budget which is devoted to military R&D.

Colin Norman of the Washington-based Worldwatch Institute, in his study on the state of science and technology in the 1980s, produced an estimate of the 1980 world R&D budget "based on data from national sources and international agencies". The figures, as Norman stresses, "are approximate and should be regarded as no more than a rough guide to relative expenditure". Norman's estimates of the 1980 global R&D budget are as follows[5]:

Programme	Share (percent)
Military	24
Basic research	15
Space	8
Energy	8
Health	7
Information processing	5
Transportation	5
Pollution control	5
Agriculture	3
Others	20
Total:	100%

Norman concludes: "the feeding of the world's military machine is thus the predominant occupation of the global R&D".[6] Yet the exact proportion of global R&D expenditures devoted to military R&D remains still a matter for further valuation; this relates mainly to the military share of basic research, space (satellites), energy (nuclear), information processing (computer science), transportation (avionics) and "others". Assuming even that only a tiny percentage of the above R&D endeavours is of a military nature, we may come to a figure of 30-35 per cent of the global R&D budget devoted in 1980 to military R&D. Given the rapid recent growth of military R&D, which, according to the Stockholm Peace Research Institute (SIPRI), amounted to at least one-third between 1980-1986,[7] the share of military R&D in total R&D may be still larger.

In 1981 the United Nations produced a comprehensive study on *The Relationship Between Disarmament and Development* with a thorough discussion of the bearing of military R&D on total R&D. Central here was the question of opportunity costs lost for development by concentration on military R&D. The study recalled that a 1972 United Nations study on *Disarmament and Development* had estimated the share of military R&D as 40 per cent of global R&D expenditures.[8] Reflecting on this estimate, the new study took a more conservative line, stating that "the most recent estimates point to a share of resources used for military R&D of the order of 20 to 25 per cent as regards both manpower and expenditure".[9] Still, the study adds, "if a more accurate accounting were possible, the figure presented above would almost certainly appear conservative."[10]

What do the above estimates mean concretely, as far as the size of world expenditures and manpower engaged in military R&D is concerned?

The 1987 *SIPRI Yearbook on World Armaments and Disarmament* calculated that "world spending on military R&D is roughly a quarter of world spending on all R&D and in 1986 was approximately US $85-100 billion a year at current prices". Moreover: "of the world's four million R&D scientists and engineers, probably over three-quarters of a million are engaged in military R&D. If support people are included, there are probably at least one and half million people in the world working in military R&D."[11] As to the national distribution of this manpower, the *SIPRI Yearbook* adds: "Two-thirds to three-quarters of all military R&D scientists and engineers are either in the USA or the USSR; more are found in the USSR, where research is more labour intensive".[12]

This may be a cautious estimate. Prof. Eugene Skolnikoff of the Massachussetts Institute of Technology has a higher assessment. Referring to R&D expenditures in 1987, he concluded:

> The funds devoted to R&D worldwide have reached astonishing proportions. No accurate tabulation is available, but a rough calculation would indicate a total of some US $400-500 billion per year. Of that amount, a reasonable estimate, probably conservative, is one-third to one-half is motivated directly or indirectly by military/security concerns.[13]

Prof. Skolnikoff divided the above estimate of global expenditure devoted to R&D into US $240 billion each for the US and USSR, US $70 billion spent in Western Europe, US $40 billion in Japan, and the remainder in the rest of the world.[14]

Thus, according to Prof. Skolnikoff, world military R&D would currently be consuming US $133-200 billion a year, or even higher: 167-250 billion. This is about twice the SIPRI estimate of the size of global expenditure for military R&D. On the other hand, the assessment of the national-geographical division of the global R&D venture is similar. SIPRI states that the world's six biggest spenders on R&D — USA, USSR, FRG, France, UK and Japan — account for some 80 per cent of world expenditure on total R&D; the six biggest spenders on military R&D, with China here replacing Japan, account for some 90-95 per cent of world expenditure, with the USA and the USSR in the mid-1980s responsible for altogether 80-84 per cent of this expenditure.[15] Characteristically, the share of major powers in military R&D is far higher than in total R&D, with the USA and the USSR, again occupying a distinctly predominant position in both manpower and expenditures.

Coming from different scholarly sources, the above computations may not be fully comparable. However, as a whole they reveal a situation in which military R&D is expanding rapidly and appropriating a lion's share of world R&D. Given the spread of military R&D in almost all disciplines and branches of science and technology — from physics, chemistry, information technology and space exploration to medicine and social sciences (so as to master war-fighting capability in all environments) — this evolution appears to mark a process of pre-emption of civilian R&D. This is done both quantitively by arrogating a massive part of resources earmarked for R&D, and qualitatively by penetrating and assuming control in key segments of total R&D.

Assuming indication of the magnitude and impact of military R&D is the share of military expenditures devoted to military R&D on the one hand, and the share of national resources earmarked for all R&D and diverted to military R&D on the other hand.

According to SIPRI, before World War II military R&D consumed on the average less than 1 per cent of the military expenditures of major powers.[16] These were themselves, in the years 1925-1938, in real value more than 10 times lower than in the 1980s.[17] But today military R&D as a percentage of military expenditure, if we take 1981-1984 averages, amounted to between 11-13 per cent of the military spending of the major Western powers: the United States, the UK and France.[18] Military R&D has become the fastest growing military expenditure item of major powers. No precise data on these and other military expenditures of the Soviet Union are available. However, there is no doubt, given the drive of the USSR to catch up and even surpass the US performance, that its outlays on military R&D are at least equal to those in the West, if not larger.

The detrimental economic and development implications of the high expenditures on military R&D come into relief when we study the data of military R&D expenditure as a percentage of all governmental outlays for R&D, civilian R&D included, and as a percentage of gross domestic expenditure on R&D. In 1981-1984, on the average, the US devoted to military R&D 60 per cent of government R&D outlays on all R&D, and 28 per cent of gross domestic expenditure on R&D.[19] The respective figures for the UK are 50 per cent and 27 per cent, and for France 38 per cent and 23 per cent.[20] A number of other countries involved in military production — from Sweden and Australia to Greece, FRG, Italy, Norway and Canada — have also followed the above trend, though at a lower level.[21] In the case of the United States, this trend seemed even to be accelerating. In 1986 the share of government R&D funds diverted to military R&D reached 72.7 per cent. While overall military R&D spending between 1981-1986 increased by 62 per cent, funding for civilian R&D in fact decreased by 10 per cent.[22]

It may be interesting to note that a developing country like India, in striving to build up its own military industry, during 1981-1984 spent on average for military R&D 26 per cent of government funds and 23 per cent of its gross domestic expenditure on R&D.[23]

Behind the above data lie structural imbalances in the allocation of resources for armaments on the one hand; and on the other hand, a drift inherent to the momentum of military R&D to amplify the weapon innovation process, thus projecting the arms race far into the future.

3.2 Armaments: a race in science-based military technology

This burgeoning expansion of military R&D has served as a powerful impulsion of armaments. It has generated a dramatic transformation in the nature and intensity of the arms race. The volume of global military expenditures between 1948 and 1985, increased five-fold in constant prices.[24] Though this escalation may also be attributed to various politico-military circumstances, a crucial role has been played by the shift in the centre of gravity of armaments: from a competition in quantities, to a rivalry in science-based military technology. The emergence of newer weapon systems has accelerated the process of obsolescence and replacement of military hardware. The eventual result was an unprecedented progress in the cost of arms and the destructive power of the war machine.

Command of the most advanced military technology has become the crucial variable of military efficiency, with qualitative superiority a central objective in the arms race. Moreover, this pursuit of qualitative advantages has trickled down, from the competition between the giants to regional and local conflicts. As the arms race has turned into a global phenomenon, its horizontal quantitative expansion has become dominated by a qualitative-vertical race. In the process, highly sophisticated conventional arms — supersonic jet fighters, armed vehicles and artillery, air-to-air and air-to-surface missiles, guidance and radar systems, and assault ships — have filled the arsenals of third world countries, finding their way to the battlefields of Asia, Africa and Latin America.[25] At the same time the proliferation of nuclear weapons and non nuclear weapon technology has acquired alarming proportions: by the 1980s not only were the nuclear stocks of the major powers saturated with stupendous quantities and a bewildering variety of nuclear explosives, but simultaneously nuclear weapon technology and know-how had spread to several "threshold countries" in politically and strategically sensitive spots of the globe — countries poised at a moment of crisis to use such acquired capability.[26] Through the impulse of high technology born in R&D laboratories, our world has become a far more dangerous place to live in. The very survival of human species is in jeopardy.

These advances in science-based military technology and their application in armaments proceeded thanks to major scientific-technological breakthroughs followed by the conjunction of different technologies in the plants of military R&D, and through the carefully pursued modernisation, improvement and refinement of new weapons and weapon systems. This mission-impelled exertion of military R&D has generated a revolution — or rather a perpetual on-going revolutionary process in the development of war, in the art of warfare and in strategic thinking.

Of the basic military scientific-technological breakthroughs of the post-World War II period, three are of monumental importance:

a) The epoch-making discovery of nuclear weapons which increased, almost infinitely, the explosive destructive power of arms;

b) the quantum/qualitative leap in the mobility and reach of modern weaponry, through the development of various high-speed intercontinental carriers of nuclear and conventional weapons, such as supersonic bombers, inter-continental ballistic missiles (ICBMs), submarine-launched ballistic missiles (SLBMs), multiple independently targetable re-entry vessels (MIRVs) and long-range cruise missiles;

c) the extension of the military thrust from land, sea and air to the near-orbit and outer-space environment, through the launching of satellites and progressive militarisation of outer space.[27]

These accomplishments in military technology were accompanied and furthered by constant progress in such specific technologies as nuclear fission techniques, microelectronics, computer sciences, solid-fuel rocketry, a wide range of sensors artificial intelligence (AI) and what is subsumed under new emerging technologies (ET).

The chief daily objective of military R&D is to operationalise the achieved knowledge in science and technology in new weapon design and development, so as to make arms more instrumental and efficient. Thus nuclear warheads underwent a basic transformation from unwieldly behemoths to versatile miniaturised versions, their weight-to-yield ratio constantly perfected; missiles were made more expedient in accuracy, speed, range, manoeuvrability, non-detectability, penetrability and target acquisition; precision-guided munitions (PGMs), in themselves a revolutionary jump, were developed and improved. Updating and uplifting the quality of arms has affected almost each of the millions of small component units of modern weapons systems.

This scientific-technological exertion has had a profound effect on the quantities and qualities of the military arsenals, especially nuclear stockpiles. Up till the late 1950s, in line with the ongoing modernisation of nuclear arms and the shift from the fission to fusion bomb, the megatonnage of nuclear stockpiles grew immensely and nuclear warheads multiplied. But from the 1960s onward, the achieved technological perfection of these weapons brought about a radical change: while operational capability was further streamlined, high redundancies were disposed of and obsolete non-functional weapons eliminated. For instance, according to official sources, the megatonnage of the US nuclear stockpile was reduced between 1960 and 1980 by a factor of four;[28] and out of 71 different types of nuclear warheads manufactured between 1945 and 1986, 42 types have been fully retired.[29] Another example was the 27 October 1983 Ottawa decision of NATO defence ministers to reduce unilaterally the European nuclear build-up by 1,400 expendable theatre and battlefield nuclear weapons.

In the light of the above, it has been asked if the December 1987 US-Soviet agreement on eliminating intermediate-range nuclear forces (INF) — important as it is from the viewpoint of improving the international political climate — was simply not one further step in the trend of getting rid of expendable weapons. On the one hand, intermediate-range nuclear weapons were aimed at targets already well covered by the many long-range ground-, air and sea-based nuclear weapons. On the other hand, the INF accord — and perhaps even further partial cuts in nuclear stockpiles — would seem to reflect more than only a trend towards redundancies-reduction. It may also reflect a re-thinking of the very war-fighting utility of nuclear weapons — weapons which by their overkill capability and massive radioactive fall-out threaten the survival of assailed and assailant alike. This has been explicitly spelled out by the policy conclusions of the January 1988 *Discriminate Deterrence* report elaborated by the Commission on Integrated Long-Term Strategy set up by the Reagan Administration. This Commission was composed of 13 high-level US strategists, including three former National Security Advisers (Henry A. Kissinger, Zbigniew Brzezinski and William A. Clark); it stated explicitly that "we cannot rely on threats expected to provoke our own annihilation if carried out . . . we must have military effective responses that can limit destruction if we are not to invite destruction of what we are defending".[30] Similar sentiments have been repeatedly aired recently by Soviet spokesmen as well

The nuclear weapons at present in the arsenals of the nuclear powers cannot possibly be used in any sound military way, nor for any sound political purpose. Moreover, in the case of INF weapons, both sides seemed uneasy about their vulnerability to false alarms, computer failure or human error. A matter for deep concern was the danger of a sudden nuclear conflagration in times of crisis which could not be brought under control with still imperfect command, control, communication and intelligence (C^3I) technologies. This, again, has been underlined in the *Discriminate Deterrence* report, which stresses that "control of space in wartime is becoming increasingly important . . . our space capabilities — critical for communication, intelligence, and control of our forces — must be made survivable or replaceable".[31]

Clearly, today the index of military power and efficiency is tabulated more in technological terms than in sheer numbers of military hardware items. Regarding nuclear arsenals, the time seems ripe for major cuts, so as, to restate the slogan of President Reagan "to render them impotent and obsolete". Yet at the same time, we should remain on guard against replacing them with technologically even more effective and ominous weapons. This may especially be the case with the SDI-impelled race to develop new generations of nuclear and exotic weapons based, as the 1972 Anti-Ballistic Missile Treaty (ABMT) so portentously foresaw, on "other physical principles".

3.3 A rush to new frontiers of military technology

Assessed from the angle of effective war-fighting capabilities in the nuclear age, two generations of military R&D accomplishments have generated in the 1980s a process of future-oriented rethinking of existing military potentials, with a view to scientific-technological refinement and enhancement of weapon systems to suit true war-fighting and war-winning objectives.[32] The main concerns of the military, the strategists and the military R&D community have centred on the vulnerabilities inherent in the devastating potential of nuclear weapons; on the absence of defence against nuclear arms; and on the constraints in the offensive potential of nuclear weapons, to attain a true war-fighting and war-winning capability by operationally combining offence and defence (in Clauswitzian tradition). Other concerns have related to scientific-technological exigencies for conventional weapons in the new military environment, and to the consequences of possible new breakthroughs in military R&D for the great-power balance of forces.

From these considerations, several new concepts have emerged as to the direction of the military scientific-technological endeavour. The greatest impact here was made by the Reagan Administration's Strategic Defence Initiative (SDI). Essentially, SDI aimed to take advantage of high-level esoteric technologies to build a space-based country-wide shield against nuclear missiles. This would mean an offence-defence strategic capacity, which also would complement nuclear and conventional offensive capabilities with space-strike weapons: a perfect scenario for a first-strike capability. Yet this "Star War" vision has met with strong criticism, especially pointing out that the SDI scheme still lies beyond the reach of available technology. In consequence, a number of derivative "strategic defence" scenarios have evolved, calling for the establishment of a ground-based anti-missile defence system to cover missile sites, command centres and other military installations: the concept of Star War II.[33]

In a typical action-reaction process, also the Soviet Union has intensified its pursuit of new technologies for ballistic missile defence based on "other physical principles". Its professed goal has been to develop cheaper counter-measures against space-strike weapons.[34] In these controversies military R&D has appeared, even within the concerned scholarly community, as a compelling hedge against the military scientific-technological race of the adversary.

Two exotic breakthrough technologies, earth- and space-based, related to "other physical principles" have become the centrepiece of a new fierce arms race: hypervelocity Kinetic Energy Weapons (KEWs) and Directed Energy Weapons (DEWs).[35] KEWs derive their destructive potential from the very speed and momentum of electromagnetic or rocket-propelled objects such as railguns or laser beams. DEWs, on the other hand, rely on high-energy chemical or nuclear-pumped X-ray lasers, and may appear in the form of particle beams of so-called radio-frequency weapons. The actual development of KEWs seems more advanced and has become the main current in SDI exertions, earmarked for deployment by the mid-1990s.[36]

In the meantime, the *Discriminate Deterrence* report, commissioned in 1986 by the Reagan Administration, provides a glimpse into the intended course of the general military scientific-technological push into the next century. The study states:

> Military technology will change substantially in the next 20 years . . . If Soviet military research continues to exceed our own, it will erode the qualitative edge on which we have long relied . . . Both our conventional and nuclear posture should be based on a mix of offensive and defensive systems . . . We need strategic defense . . . We need a

capability for conventional counter-offensive operations deep into enemy territory . . . We and our allies need to exploit emerging technologies of precision, control, and intelligence that can provide our conventional forces with more selective and more effective capabilities for destroying military targets . . . We will need capabilities for discriminate nuclear strikes . . .

Carefully designed reductions in nuclear arms could lead to a safer balance of offensive and defensive forces . . . We must maintain a mix of survivable stategic offensive arms and command and control capabilities . . .

In the Third World, no less than in developed countries, US strategy should seek to maximise our technological advantages . . . Here too we will want to use smart missiles that can apply force in a discriminate fashion and avoid collateral damage to civilians . . .[37]

And in a special chapter on "Managing Technology", stressing the programmes of "highest priority" to widen the options to future US Presidents, the study continues:

We would assign a high priority — higher than it has been getting in recent years — to spending in the accounts for basic research and advanced development. Among the programs meeting these criteria, four seem especially urgent:
1. the integration of "low-observable" (Stealth) systems into our force structure;
2. "smart" weapons — precision-guided munitions that combine range and high accuracy;
3. ballistic missile defense; and
4. space capabilities needed for wartime operations . . .[38]

In sum, the study envisages the pursuit of futuristic technologies, including SDI ballistic missile and space technologies, to arrive at a nuclear-conventional and offensive-defensive war-fighting and war-winning capability — and thus on a global scale. It envisages "discriminate" nuclear strikes, military operations deep into the territories of the adversary and "discriminate" war-fighting in the Third World.

In operational terms, as a military correspondent of the *International Herald Tribune* puts it, the study postulates that

the West should concentrate on high-technology weapons capable of delivering nuclear strikes and move away from weapons that threaten nuclear Armageddon (i.e.) without triggering a massive reprisal.

Moreover,

the report presses the case for new technology be saying that missiles can be accurate enough for conventional warheads to provide the same long-range capabilities as nuclear weapons do now.[39]

The above blueprint for "discriminate" war-fighting, charting the course of military technology into the 21st century, in fact means projecting ongoing military R&D into the future. As such, given the current parallel course in the exertions of military laboratories, and the correspondence of high-tech military deployments by US/USSR, and in view of the absence of Soviet publications on the nature and trends in the Soviet military-technological endeavour, the US scheme can be seen as marking the general direction of the East-West technological arms race, with possible future modifications.

The process should be perceived not in static but in highly dynamic terms of the technological race. While negotiations are proceeding for "careful designed reductions in nuclear arms" (as stated in the *Discriminate Deterrence* report), military R&D laboratories East and West are working full speed to achieve new technological breakthroughs, to design, develop and produce new types of weapons and weapon systems. Again, by default of Soviet openness in this domain, US pieces of information are indicative. Thus the *U.S. News & World Report* stated in autumn 1987:

> Over the next three years, nearly 50 major weapon systems are scheduled to move from prototype to production . . .

And further:

> Since 1981, military research and development has grown twice as fast as overall Pentagon spending . . . According to the House Armed Services Committee, every dollar for military R&D generates about $10 in subsequent defense spending . . . Pentagon planners concede that early orders for 47 new weapon systems expected to come on line during the next five years will cost more than $150 million . . . In the next five years, more than a half-dozen aircraft are scheduled to begin production . . . New generations of strategic missiles — including Trident 2 D-5 and the single warhead Midgetman — are also in the pipeline . . . The Pentagon puts so much into R&D that nobody can back out of it . . .[40]

These developments are seldom fully open to public view. Whenever concern about the race in military technology is voiced, military R&D is justified by arguments of national security. There follow then odd additional contentions that military R&D is beneficial for arms control since it produces better tools for arms control and verification, and that it actually has contributed to reduction in nuclear megatonnage and types of weapon systems.

There is, of course, some truth in such artful argumentations. However, like all half-truths, this tends to obscure basic reality. Obviously, national security is not enhanced but weakened by the spiralling arms build-up. Nor do the massive military R&D investments and constant new inventions in intelligence — be they different kinds of spy satellites, sensor technologies or C³I installations — hardly serve the arms control exercise: on the contrary, they stimulate the arms race and tend to perfect war-fighting capabilities. And concerning the reduction of nuclear arsenals, as we have seen, this has gone hand-in-hand with progress in their efficiency.

The race in modern military technology has a distinct destabilising effect on the military environment, as well as marring the climate of international relations. The pursuit of technological "fixes" for arms control only clouds over the need for genuine disarmament and for political solutions to our arms race predicament.

3.4 Military R&D and armaments dynamics

The foregoing analysis of the quantitative and qualitative aspects of the militarisation of R&D indicates the extent and role of military R&D in fuelling armaments and sustaining the momentum of the arms race.

Contemporary armaments dynamics in the East-West context are a multi-dimensional and multi-casual phenomenon. From the perspective of the military competition between the superpowers, there is mutual stimulation between the internal and external motor forces of the arms race, as expressed in action-reaction or mirror image paradigms (illustrated below):

Action ⟵⟶ Reaction

In the Superpower Competition

Nuclear Weapons

US 1945	atomic bomb	1949 USSR
US 1946	electronic computer	1951 USSR
US 1948	intercontinental bomber	1955 USSR
US 1952	thermonuclear bomb	1953 USSR
USSR 1957	intercontinental ballistic missile (ICBM)	1958 US
USSR 1957	man-made satellite	1958 US
USSR 1958	early-warning radar	1960 US
US 1960	submarine-launched ballistic missile (SLBM)	1968 USSR
US 1966	multiple warhead (MRV)	1968 USSR
USSR 1968	anti-ballistic missile (ABM)	1972 US
US 1970	multiple independently-targeted warhead (MIRV)	1975 USSR
USSR 1971	sea-launched cruise missile	1982 US
US 1983	neutron bomb	199? USSR
US 1985	new strategic bomber	1987 USSR
USSR 1987	single warhead, mobile ICBM	1992 US
US 1990?	stealth bomber	199? USSR

Conventional Weapons

USSR 1949	main battle tank	1952 US
US 1955	nuclear-powered submarine	1958 USSR
US 1955	large-deck aircraft carrier	1975 USSR
USSR 1955	wire-guided anti-tank missile	1972 US
US 1959	photo reconnaissance satellite	1962 USSR
US 1960	supersonic bomber	1975 USSR
US 1960	computer-guided missile	1968 USSR
US 1961	nuclear-powered aircraft carrier	1992 USSR
USSR 1961	surface-to-air missile	1963 US
US 1962	long-range fighter bomber	1973 USSR
US 1964	air-to-surface missile	1968 USSR
USSR 1970	high-speed attack submarine	1976 US
US 1972	television-guided missile	1987 USSR
USSR 1972	heavy attack helicopter	1982 US
US 1975	jet-propelled combat aircraft	1983 USSR
US 1976	large amphibious assault ship	1978 USSR
USSR 1978	multiple-launch rocket system	1983 US
US 1987	binary (chemical) weapons	199? USSR

Source: Ruth Leger Sivard, *World Military and Social Expenditure 1987-88.*

However, from a broader methodological point of view, taking into account economic, socio-political and systemic factors, we must differentiate between underlying structural determinants on the one hand, and a set of cogent behavioural-doctrinal and functional determinants to the arms race on the other hand.[41] These correspond roughly to the dialectical relationship between the material base and ideological-functional superstructure, where the structural determinants match the substantial material base and the behavioural-doctrinal and functional determinants are akin to the reciprocally reactive phenomenon in the attitudinal and operational superstructure.

Two primary motor forces are at work, the first one is the management of the political economy of armaments, dominated by what has been subsumed as the military-industrial complex, i.e. the socio-political corporate constituencies most interested and involved in the procurement of arms; these include the military, the military industry and, increasingly, the state-political bureaucracy with its keen interest in armaments as an instrument of policy and diplomacy (which is obviously true for both the East and West). The second major force here is the uninterrupted forceful exertion of military R&D.

These two structural forces interact in a reciprocal way: the technological allure of power from the military laboratories activates the various armament constituencies in pursuit of more and better arms: and vice versa, the executives of armaments constituencies relate back to military R&D their specific requirements for the assortments of arms. The actual interplay between these two fundamental arms race determinants is essentially a problem of the chicken and the egg. At technological breakthrough junctures — such as the pursuit and development of nuclear weapons — the scientific-technological community generally takes the lead; on the other hand, requirements for improvements and modernisation of weapons, if not the outcome of the laboratory R&D momentum, often come from the armaments constituencies as well.

On the superstructural level, the arms race is nurtured by ideological dogma, perceptional and attitudinal asymmetries, as well as by personal idiosyncrasies of individual leaders. A potent stimulus comes today from rigid military doctrines such as nuclear deterrence. This is a speculative tenet with no hard evidence to validate or invalidate it. However, it possesses a ring of plausibility — although the historical record of deterrence theories like "si vis pacem para bellum" (if you desire peace, prepare for war) is unequivocal: in the long run this doctrine has served not to preserve peace but to sustain preparation for war, not infrequently leading to war.

Figure 7
Great-Power Armaments Dynamics

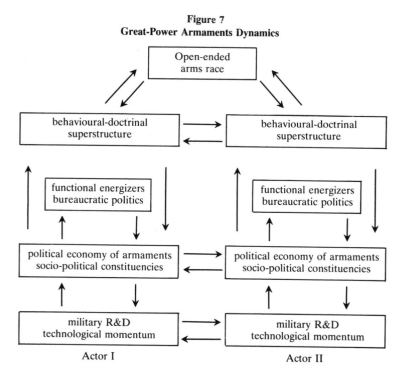

Between the structural base and the doctrinal-behavioural superstructure lie functional energisers of the arms race. Chief among them we find bureaucratic politics combined with institutional inertia; this is reflected in the way the arms flow is amplified in the protracted competitive process from the laboratory, through production until acquisition and deployment. In a mix of clashes and compromises between the various corporate armaments constituencies, including the three branches of the armed forces, the number and varieties of weapons are levelled up to the highest common denominator.

As totality, armament dynamics are highly influenced by the thrust of modern science-based military technology. different ingredients of military technology and the impulse from military R&D permeate all aspects and levels of the base and superstructure of the armaments momentum: the structural, behavioural-doctrinal and functional corridors of the arms race. In particular, military R&D too often acts to pre-empt the political decision-making process. By sketching captivating technological visions of force-aggrandisement, and expounding narrow, one-directional options at moments of decisions, military technologists actually leave the decision-makers with little alternative choice.[42] A good recent example of the influence exerted by hawkish sections of the military scientific-technological community on the political decision-making process can be seen in the circumstances of the launching of the Strategic Defence Initiative. As is now widely known, the inspiration for SDI came from the military laboratories.[43]

Assessed in its entirety, the impact of military R&D on the arms race emanates not only from its quantitative weight — the million or more best qualified scientists and engineers employed by military R&D, and the hundreds of billions of dollars feeding annually the military laboratories East and West — but more so from the tight institutional set-up close to the seats of power, and its mode of operation that invigorates and perpetuates the arms race. Military R&D is a prestigious establishment, the "tail that wags the armaments dog".[44]

We need to perceive clearly the work regularities and operational imperatives of military R&D. These are embedded:

— in the years- and decades- long lead-times and gestation periods of research, design, development, repeated testing, prototype production and product improvement that infuse constancy and petrify the arms race; the moment a long-haul new weapon project is undertaken, and corporate support behind it builds up, any withdrawal becomes extremely difficult, even should the weapon prove faulty (cf. the history of the MX missile and the B1 bomber);

— in the "follow-on imperative" driven by scientific curiosity, ambitional cravings and professional routine, requiring the pursuit of excellence and constant perfection of produced materials; this also requires alternating the development of arms offence with arms of defence and vice versa, on the assumption that the adversary is certain to acquire similar or even better weapons; the result is to end up racing against one's own achievements. Evidently, more than in other domains of R&D, military R&D is conscious of requirements for high-tech performance, with the very R&D process becoming a continuum without any specific end to the scientific-technological exertion and with little regard for the costs involved. No new opening can be left unheeded and new venues have to be sought with utmost vigour; each new stage in the R&D endeavour becomes a starting point for a fresh departure to yet another round in the arms spiral. There is a self-stimulating effect in the "follow-on-imperative"; the more advanced the technological race, the greater the reliance on military R&D. Consequently, military R&D itself has a propensity to grow and intensify its prowess;

— in worst-case projections and planning, far beyond prudent assessment of the achievements and capabilities of the adversary. Part of this propensity stems from the general secretiveness of the armaments endeavour, further intensified by the nervousness, fear and uncertainty that pervade technological competition. This then generates the urge to pre-emption, to over-design and over-reaction — a drive out of proportion with real challenges; it institutionalises excess.

All of the above operational imperatives of military R&D meet and intertwine. The synergetic effect is to routinise and petrify the thrust of the arms race. The non-synchronised efforts of R&D in East and West, reinforced by perceptional asymmetries, amplify this momentum. Cycles of moves and countermoves, crossing each other in unexpected ways, put their imprint on the arms race. Weapons in the armouries of today are thought to be obsolete, while those on the drawing boards project the arms race into the future.

Trying to depict the arms race drive generated by military R&D, the scientific community has coined the term "technological imperative". By this is meant, as formulated by W. Panofsky, that "new technology tends to generate its own momentum".[45] Anatol Rapoport has defined the technological imperative as follows:

> The technological imperative can be seen as a massive compulsion to engage the full potential of scientific knowledge in the service of the war machine. The compulsion is inherent in the self-propelling dynamics of

burgeoning technological progress. The ever-increasing complexity of weapons systems necessitates a further increase in the complexity of the supporting systems, which, in turn, creates opportunities for making weapon systems even more sophisticated . . . When we consider that by analogy with similar processes in othe fields of endeavour, the burgeoning complexity of weapon systems is conceived as 'progress', we realise how strong are the pressures for escalation.[46]

Expansion is inherent in the very nature of military R&D. The uninterrupted innovative process of military R&D generates abundancies of weapons and weapon systems. In it lies the push which has produced the enormous redundancies in the nuclear arsenal.[47] This innovative process is also responsible for weapon systems which have "evolved without a well-defined conception of why they were needed, and without an assessment of their full implications," as was the case with the emergence of long-range cruise missiles and MIRVs.[48]

In sum, no matter how contemporary armament dynamics are conceived in theory and however they are described in their multi-casual complexity, we must recognise the central role of the running drive of military R&D. High military technology dominates priorities in the arms race. Military R&D has become the crucial variable in armament dynamics. As stated in the UN study on the relationship between disarmament and development:

> One of the most conspicuous distinguishing features of the military scene since the Second World War has been the extraordinarily rapid rate of change in weapon technology. It is this feature of the post-war arms race that is primarily responsible for the unique intensity of this race.[49]

4. Impact of military technology on economic development

There is a *sui generis* conflictual relationship between military science and technology, and human development. It is not only that military and civilian R&D are competing for the same finite human and material resources. At a deeper structural level, military R&D and the resultant military technology evince operational peculiarities which inhibit rather than promote economic development. This holds true for the economic performance of developed countries engaged in the arms race, and even more so for developing nations.

Three traits of military technology are of particular importance:
a) a propensity to, and keen pursuit of, the highest and most sophisticated technology, not suitable for civilian production;
b) an inherent capital-intensiveness and operation virtually without regard to production costs; and
c) an addiction to excessive secretiveness.

As has become clearly evident in studies on economic conversion,[50] experience has shown that the high-tech performance criteria commonly applied to military products do not fit civilian industry. High technologically-intensive production and implements are simply not geared to a civilian consumption economy. The weight of this state of affairs and its negative implications can be perceived in the fact that today the importance of science-based technology for economic performance is much higher than that of capital and labour. Moreover, technological change tends to accelerate exponentially leaving behind those weaker and less resourceful segments of the national and international economy unable to keep pace or catch up with technological mobility and oscillation. This is a special drawback for developing countries. Perceptibly, military technology exerts an influence on the nature of civilian technology. It "affects the choices and conduct of research in the universities, industry and national laboratories."[51]

As well as leaning towards technological-intensiveness, military R&D and military technology are also highly capital-intensive, the two being in the very mode of operation of military R&D. We may note this in the trend in military R&D to reduce yesterday's distance between basic and applied research — basic research being today contrived in the huge military laboratories with an eye to actual employment. The intention is to shorten to maximum lead-times in the R&D process. In a sense, time is bought by the inpouring of capital. Again, the capital-intensiveness of military and military-inspired high technology hits the developing countries most severely. As observed by Prof. Vassily Leontief of Columbia University: "Critical shortage of investment funds is now and will for a long time be the central problem of the so-called developing areas."[52] And further: "Introduction of the new technologies, diminishing the growth of human labour as the principal factor of production, is bound to weaken the competitive position of the populous third world countries."[53] But developed countries are also harmed. The appropriation of a lion's share of human and material resources by military R&D rebounds, in a shortage of these resources for civilian R&D. Consequently, productivity and economic performance of the civilian economy must suffer.

The inordinate secretiveness of military R&D and the military scientific-technological drive has a profoundly detrimental impact on development and, indeed, on civilisational progress. As long as security is perceived largely in terms of military hardware, a certain degree of confidentiality in armaments may be considered unavoidable. However, in the field of military R&D, secretiveness has now not only exceeded the bounds of real precaution, but has come to be part and parcel of the scientific-technological endeavour itself. In the process, it has proven counterproductive to the very pursuit of both science and security.

The harm done by the undue secretiveness of the military scientific-technological drive extends to almost all spheres of productive activity and human cultural-scholarly undertaking. In relation to development, secrecy imposed by military R&D tends to stretch its veil over all R&D by limiting the flow of information and of the scientific-technological discourse. At the same time, military R&D, with all its high-tech secrets, isolates itself from the rest of the scientific-technological pursuit. Moreover, it tries actively to withhold information on perceived "sensitive" R&D carried out by civilian sector. There is some contagious effect on civilian R&D itself. Fearing a military buy-up or military-inspired classification of its processes because of perceived potential military application, civilian R&D may tend to hold back publication of its own achievements.

At a deeper level, the secrecy practiced by military R&D challenges the very ethos of creative science. After all, the latter professes principles of openness, a free flow of information, shared knowledge and communication within the scientific community — and, indeed, with society at large — as a fundamental credo and law of inventive and fertile scientific pursuit. Secrecy within the scientific-technological domain thus acts to corrupt and stifle all scientific advance.

Finally, in questions of defence, such secrecy can have dire consequences for genuine security: on one hand it obscures the security dilemmas facing society, including part of the decision-makers (such as members of the legislature) thus foreclosing clear judgements in the security domain, and eventually preventing discrimination in the use/misuse of science and technology, in the name of security; and on the other hand, it tends to augment insecurity by stimulating suspicion and mistrust among nations.

Hence, it is of cardinal importance for true human development to lower the veil of secrecy and confidentiality in the realm of military scientific-technological exertion. This is intimately linked to questions of peace and war.

4.1 Implications for developed countries engaged in the arms race
For lack of reliable data on the extent of Soviet military R&D and studies on the interrelationship between the drive in military technology and economic performance in the USSR, we will here have to concentrate mainly on the impact of military technology on economic development in the major Western nations. We must assume that the consequences of the race in military technology and

Table 5
Military and Civil R&D Expenditure
Military R&D (MIRD), civil government R&D (civil GOVRD) and gross domestic R&D (GERD) expenditure as percentage shares of gross domestic product (GDP), 3-year averages 1961-1984

	1961-63	1964-66	1967-69	1970-72	1973-75	1976-78	1979-81	1982-84
USA								
MIRD	1.32	1.09	0.97	0.79	0.67	0.62	0.62	0.80
civil GOVRD	0.62	0.97	0.89	0.70	0.60	0.63	0.62	0.45
GERD	NA	3.06	3.02	2.66	2.42	2.36	2.46	2.73
Japan								
MIRD	0.01	0.01	0.01	NA	0.01	0.01	0.01	0.01
civil GOVRD	0.45	0.49	0.48	NA	0.58	0.58	0.61	0.62
GERD	1.31	1.31	1.52	1.93	2.03	1.99	2.23	2.40
Fed. Rep. of Germany								
MIRD	0.12	0.16	0.19	0.15	0.14	0.13	0.12	0.11
civil GOVRD	0.49	0.65	0.75	0.93	1.07	0.98	1.03	1.05
GERD	NA	1.51	1.77	2.16	2.16	2.19	2.44	2.58
France								
MIRD	0.42	0.53	0.46	0.34	0.36	0.34	0.43	0.46
civil GOVRD	0.59	0.87	1.01	0.84	0.80	0.72	0.74	0.92
GERD	1.58	1.98	2.11	1.89	1.79	1.76	1.89	2.15
UK								
MIRD	0.78	0.73	0.56	0.52	0.58	0.61	0.68	0.63
civil GOVRD	0.52	0.60	0.67	0.75	0.79	0.67	0.69	0.69
GERD	NA	2.36	2.33	2.12	2.18	2.19	2.42	2.27

Source: Unpublished SIPRI worksheets based on OECD, EC and official national sources. An appendix to Mary Acland-Hood: "Military and civil R&D expenditure", *Science and Public Policy*, Vol.13, No.1, February 1986, p.54.

Figure 8
Military R&D expenditures as percentage share of GDP, 1961-1984

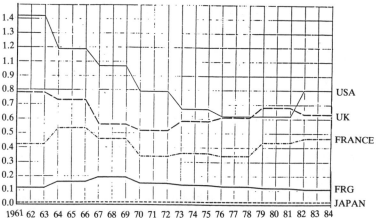

Source: Table 5.

Table 6
Civil R&D expenditures as percentage share of GDP
(Gross domestic R&D as percentage of GDP minus military R&D as percentage of GDP)

	1964-66	1967-69	1970-72	1973-75	1976-78	1979-81	1982-84
USA	1.97	2.05	1.87	1.75	1.74	1.84	1.93
Japan	1.30	1.51	1.92	2.02	1.98	2.22	2.39
FRG	1.35	1.58	2.01	2.02	2.06	2.32	2.47
France	1.16	1.45	1.65	1.43	1.42	1.27	1.69
UK	1.63	1.77	1.60	1.60	1.58	1.74	1.64

Source: Computed from Table 4.

Figure 9
Civil R&D expenditures as percentage share of GDP, 1964-1984

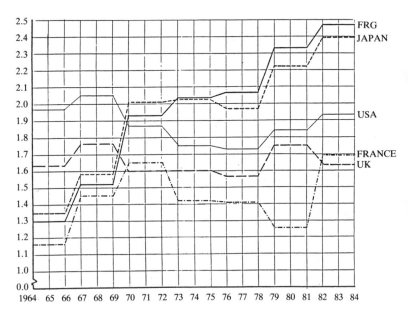

Source: Table 6.

armaments are of a similar nature in East and West. As observed by Prof. Lloyd J. Dumas of the University of Texas: "The use of productive resources (labour, materials, capital, fuel, etc.) for non-productive purposes constitutes a drain on the vitality and prosperity of any economy."[54]

The predicaments of the highly militarised Soviet economy are well known, and the *perestroika* attempt by Secretary-General Gorbachev is evidence of efforts to come to grips with the stagnation and deteriorating economic performance. A substantial part of these problems stem from the militarisation of the scientific-technological exertion, particularly the preemption of civilian economic operability through the priority attached to maximising military technology.

To get some insight into the impact of priority investments in military R&D and military technology as against preference in civilian R&D and technology, we may try to compare the economic performance of the major Western nations high or low in military, respectively civilian R&D. Table 5 shows longitudinal trends in the United States, Japan, the Federal Republic of Germany, France and the United Kingdom.

The data should be self-explanatory:
— In military R&D expenditures, as percentage share of GDP, the United States holds a leading position, followed by the UK and France; on the other pole indicating low military R&D expenditures as percentage share of GDP, we find Japan and the FRG. The discrepancy between the United States and Japan as well as the FRG is striking; in the 1982-1984 period, the US spent on military R&D 0.80 per cent of its GDP while the corresponding figure for Japan was 0.01 per cent and for the FRG 0.11 per cent.
— There has been fluctuation in US military R&D expenditures over the years. The peak occurred in the 1960s, which were marked by the vigorous expansion of military technology with the development of ICBMs, SLBMs, MIRVs, long-range cruise missiles, a variety of nuclear warheads and the launching of military satellites. We note yet another rise in the 1980s, linked to the SDI and the extension of the arms race into outer space.
— Concerning civilian R&D expenditures, two sets of indicators deserve attention: a) government funding of civil R&D, and b) total civil R&D expenditures, i.e. government plus private investments (percentage share of GDP minus MIRD — see table 6). In the first case, the US exhibits a high preponderance of military R&D over government funded civil R&D, whereas Japan and FRG have promoted overwhelmingly civil government R&D over military R&D. France has favoured civil government R&D to a lesser extent, and the UK has divided support equally for military and civil R&D. In the second case, with total civil R&D expenditures as percentage share of GDP, there are also remarkable disparities between nations high and low in the arms race: while in the 1982-1984 period the US equivalent of total civil R&D expenditure as share of GDP was 1.93 per cent, the corresponding indicator for the FRG was 2.47

per cent, for Japan 2.39 per cent, for France 1.69 per cent and for the UK 1.64 per cent. Again Japan and the FRG surpassed the US, and even more France and the UK, in their concern for civilian R&D.

— Noteworthy is the fact that while government funding for civilian R&D in the US indicates some decline from the 1960s onwards, during the same period Japan almost doubled its government expenditures on civilian R&D, and the FRG energetically moved ahead in the same direction. Also France seemed to attach greater importance to civilian R&D, while in the UK government remained almost equally divided between military and civilian R&D.

The above data should be taken as indicators of priorities in R&D investments. In absolute monetary value, the order of magnitudes and the differences are much higher, because US Gross Domestic Product was 2.8 times greater than that of Japan and 1.7 times that of FRG, France and the UK taken together.[55] Accordingly, in cash value the US alone spent on military R&D four times as much as UK, France and Japan taken together. The high priority accorded in the United States to military R&D as against civil R&D appears to have been one of the main reasons for a retardation of the growth-rate of civilian-related technology with "a slowing down of the nations's productivity growth, even to the vanishing point".[56] It greatly reduced US competitiveness on international markets, at the same time as Japan and the FRG exhibited a dynamic growth in economic productivity and performance.

Some of the consequences for the United States are listed in a 1987 economic account by *US News & World Report* entitled "Will the US Stay Number One?". The report cites the following facts:

— World business executives surveyed by the European Management Forum, a Swiss research firm, rate the US as only the fifth most competitive nation. Topping the list are Japan and Germany.

— Japan has taken over 47 per cent of world sales of semiconductor chips.

— Over 70 per cent of the value of components in an IBM personal computer is made in Japan and Singapore.

— As recently as 1981, the US was shipping nearly 43 per cent of the world's computers. By 1985, the share had dropped to just over 34 per cent

— The share of the US market held by foreign goods rose between 1981 and 1986 from 59 per cent to 66 per cent in TVs and radios, from 33 per cent to 63 per cent in shoes, from 27 per cent to 45 per cent in machine tools, from 27 per cent to 28 per cent in cars and from 7 per cent 25 per cent in computers.

— Not a single factory manufactures home videocassette recorders, one of today's hottest consumer electronic items.
— More than 60 percent of industrial robots installed in US factories in 1986 have come from Japan. At latest count, the US had more than 14,000 robots in use, compared with 67,000 in Japan.

US News & World Report concludes: "Help would come, many experts believe, if the nation would establish policies that pump more funds into civilian research and development, regardless of commitments considered vital for military research and development."[57]

Some of the root cause of the setbacks in the US economy related to the imbalance between military and civilian technology have been summarised by John Tirman of the Union of Concerned Scientists. In the conclusion to the collection of studies on "Militarisation of High Technology" Tirman makes the following points:

— as defence and military technology today have a dominant influence on the kind of activities conducted in US research centres, they exert a strong impact on the totality of R&D, skewing, however subtly, the intent and conduct of a wide variety of research and development projects.
— military technology too often negatively affects the course of technological development; a case in point is the fate of commercial nuclear power where designs fostered by the US Navy led to "a wholesale economic disaster compared with the widely held expectations for the technology"[58]; likewise aerospace consciously divided into a civilian and military effort with little technology sharing between the two, and more attention accorded to the military effort, led to military predominance in space science and a drain of technical talent to the weapons effort;
— military technology specification of a far greater precision or of a wholly different nature than do commercial technologies, so as to withstand extreme temperatures, motion, radioactivity and so forth; the trouble with such requirements is not merely their limited applicability to commercial enterprise, but that entire industries tend to be afflicted with "overdevelopment", with the US aviation industry a prime case;
— high priority attached to military technology affects technological development in many ways: it makes itself felt in trade imbalances, inflationary trends, the nature of labour market, employment, and "deskilling" through the vigorous pursuit of automated manufacturing technologies.[59]

The current economic predicaments of the United States have many roots. Yet one of the prime causes clearly lies in the militarisation of the economy and technology. The twofold sequel to such militarisation is an impairment of the productive potential of society, and the misuse of science and technology for perfecting tools of war.

4.2 The "spin-off" myth

Whenever the economic utility of military R&D is questioned, voices can still be heard attributing it to a considerable developmental 'spin-off' value.

Of course, it canot be denied that some spillover from military to civilian R&D does occur. Indeed, it would be rather strange if in circumstances of such massive investments in military R&D no spillover to the civilian sector should take place. Such spinoffs have been noted especially in the dual-use technologies such as computer sciences, avionics, semiconductor devices or electronics. However, the questions to ask are these: what are the opportunity costs of such roundabout exploits, what are the alternative benefits foregone and the price paid for the relatively limited gains? Is looking for spinoffs from military undertakings the most effective way to pursue economic progress? And, most of all, would not direct investment in civilian R&D be more profitable and produce better results?

Though with some commonsense reasoning the answer to those questions would seem self-evident, a precise weighing of the balance of gains and losses may not be easy. It may be especially difficult to quantify the share of military R&D resources actually converted into civilian benefits foregone by economically unproductive investments, not to mention the damage of the detrimental impact on overall economic performance by the militarisation of technology. However, one approach is to assess the interplay between military and civilian R&D in their totality, taking into account both quantity and quality.

Though much in the interplay between military and civilian R&D would point to spinoffs going in both directions, several rational arguments and empirical evidence strongly indicate that the main trend is for spillovers not *from* the military to civilian, but rather in the opposite direction: from civilian to military R&D.

First, the spinoff interplay is not an inert relationshiip. It involves an interaction of power. From this point of view, military R&D is certainly the stronger partner, bent to make use of civilian R&D for its purpose. Military R&D has acquired a controlling position in the totality of R&D endeavour, civilian R&D included. It is a well-knit undertaking, rich in resources, homogenous and highly mission-conscious, under special government patronage. It has ramifications not only in almost all scientific and technological bids but also in most industrial and economic activity. Military R&D has keen insight into what is brewing in openly conducted civilian R&D, and has a reach that facilitates intervention and taking hold of what it may perceive to be of interest and use for the military. The reverse is obviously not true: civilian R&D has but a rather low awareness of developments in military R&D. Actually, the take-over of civilian technology by military R&D is proceeding systematically, with military R&D regularly monitoring and checking emerging technologies in the totality of R&D and buying up the most promising projects from civilian undertakings.

Second, the spinoff interplay between military and civilian R&D relates also to quality: to an interaction between a high-tech performance of military technology and a less-sophisticated consumer technology. Concerning the qualitative-technological grip, military R&D is definitely better equipped than civilian R&D. It is then only natural that military R&D should be in a position to bend the current of know-how from the lower to the higher layers of technological excellence. There is much less compulsion, objective impulse or utility to give away high-tech experience to more rudimentary endeavours. In most cases, high-tech military technology is simply unsuitable and of little use for daily-use technology. *SIPRI Yearbook 1987* notes in this respect: "The increasing specialisation of military technology make the probablility of civil spinoff less and less likely. Moreover, what spinoffs there are occur not only from military to civil uses but also vice versa."[60]

In some cases where civilian technology has borrowed from military R&D, as in avionics, the outcome has been rather detrimental for the civilian enterprise. The result has been long-term dependence and, as indicated above, a "baroque" way of engineering with a lasting harmful effect.[61] At the same time, military R&D is not only in a better position to make use of advanced civilian technology; it also systematically intercepts and buys off young and promising scientists and engineers, causing a brain drain from the civil sector both at home and abroad.

Finally, the United States and the Western powers have explicitly recognised the liability and potentialities inherent in the flow and use of civilian technology for military purposes. This is evident in their imposing through the Coordination Committee on Multilateral Exports (COCOM), tough restrictions for the export of "sensitive" civilian technology to the Soviet Union and other socialist countries.

Less known is the fact that many technological achievements now associated with military R&D have in fact originated in civilian

R&D. Thus "the transitor was developed in 1948 by Bell Labs and then sold to the military. Texas Instruments patented the integrated circuit in 1959 without military funds. Mostek developed the first single calculator chip in 1969 and Intel the first microprocessor in 1972, all without government funding."[62] This fits well with the historical experience of the utilisation by the military of advanced manufacturing technologies beginning from the 19th century to World War II onward.

With the flow of technology between the civil and military sectors today much greater than 20-30 years ago, it is even more probable that the real spillover is much more intense from the civilian to the military than from the military to the civilian sectors. Indeed, this is in fact recognised in the scholarly community.[63] A study of the US National Academy of Engineering on "Technology Transfer and Utilisation" observed with reference to military R&D that "with few exceptions, the vast technology developed by federally funded programmes since World War II has not resulted in widespread 'spinoffs' of secondary or additional applications of practical products, processes and services that have made an impact on the nation's economic growth, industrial productivity, employment gains, and foreign trade."[64]

The spinoffs in R&D are overwhelmingly civilian-military rather than military-civilian is implicitly admitted by the US Administration. Calling for openness in research on superconductivity, Prof. Robert L. Park of the American Physical Society writes: "Mr. Reagan's own Commission on Industrial Competitiveness, in its 1985 report, concluded that the Department of Defense is a 'net consumer' of new technologies. What it was saying was that military development relies on spin-off from civilian research — and not the other way around."[65]

It should be evident that this indirect way, whether intentional or not, of feeding civilian technology by bulky investments in military R&D is ineffective and wasteful. The straightforward way, without interposed capital-avid and high-tech military R&D, is logically the most productive and successful. The case of the Japanese Human Frontier Programme administered by Japan's Ministry of International Trade and Industry (MITI) and the Science Technology Agency (STA) is instructive.[66] With high priorities in military R&D, the US is visibly losing its economic competitiveness to Japanese industry, which has staked on civilian-oriented R&D. According to President Reagan's Commission on Industrial Competitiveness, over the past 20 years, 7 out of 10 US technology-oriented industries have lost ground in the world markets.[67]

Both rational analysis and empirical evidence show that the "spinoff" theory sees military R&D as a profitable and expedient manner of buttressing civilian technologies is but a myth. Nurtured by the military-industrial constituencies, it is indeed a make-believe myth based on half-truths, trying to blur reality: namely, that military R&D is an uneconomical and unreliable complex that retards economic progress and human development.

4.3 Sustaining North-South development polarisation

Relative to developed countries, the problems posed by the use and misuse of science and technology are in the developing countries far more consequential and more acute. Even more than in developed countries, the technological-development variable governs the internal socio-economic predicaments and relations with the rest of the world. In comparison to the developed nations, the developing countries are a veritable desert when it comes to science and technology. With a population over three times as large but a GNP less than a quarter of that of the developed world,[68] the developing countries are to the extreme exposed to the scarcities of science and technology with all the consequences this situation has for underdevelopment.

At the same time, the developing countries have been made to feel keenly the brunt of the arms race fuelled by military R&D. While the major powers have been competing in the expansion of the military build-up in East and West, the centre of gravity of armed conflict and war, with no small instigation by the world powers, has shifted to the continents of Asia, Africa and Latin America. Since World War II until the end of 1984, a total of 159 wars have taken place on these continents, with 30 yet still raging;[69] and most of the weapons for these 159 wars have been supplied by the major powers. In the process, as a percentage of GNP, developing countries have spent no less on military expenditures than have the developed countries — with a declining trend in the developed world and a rising trend in developing nations. Between 1960 and 1986, the GNP percentage spent on military expenditure by developed countries declined from 7 per cent to 5.7 per cent, whereas in the developing countries this share increased from 3.1 per cent to 5.4 per cent.[70] Also as percentage of world military expenditure, the share of developing countries has in the same period risen sharply: from 7 per cent in 1960 to 19.3 per cent by 1986.[71] Moreover, a dollar spent on weapons by a developing country has in economic terms a far higher value than one spent by a developed nation. Further, arms purchased by the Third World contributed considerably to their indebtedness. "Had they made no foreign arms purchases during the period 1972-1982, non-oil developing countries would have needed to borrow an estimated 20 per cent less each year and their accumulated debts by the end of the period would have been roughly 15 per cent smaller."[72]

A number of structural features related to the working of military and civilian R&D on a global scale underlie underdevelopment in the Third World. These create a developmental threshold which it will be difficult to transcend in the foreseeable future, unless radical transformation of the world economic and military order can be undertaken.

First comes the North-South maldistribution of human and material resources devoted to R&D. This discrepancy tends not to diminish but to increase. An African UNESCO conference in 1974 set as its goal to increase by 1980 the number of research scientists in Africa to 200 per million inhabitants. As we have seen, by 1980 there were still only 86 scientists and engineers per million population in Africa.[73]

This reflects a stagnation which has become part of agricultural decay, environmental degradation and hunger in many parts of the African continent.

The global maldistribution of R&D is ingrained in the fabric and dynamics of military R&D. Dominated by high-tech military R&D, total global R&D evinces little interest in developing problems of the Third World. It is geared to military and industrial requirements of the developed countries, whereas what the Third World needs is intermediate and appropriate technology adapted to specific socio-economic conditions, cultural habits and traditional ways of life of developing nations. The capital-intensive and labour-saving technologies sought after by the developed countries are antithetic to developed essentials in the Third World.

Second, in larger third world countries, such as India, Brazil and Egypt, science and technology tend to appear on the scene in association with military R&D, with a considerable part of R&D funds devoted to military purposes. As we have seen, in India the share of government R&D devoted to military R&D in 1981-84 was 26 per cent. Coming at the sensitive time of the take-off period in development, this conjunction tends, even more than in developed countries, to impinge on the nature and trends in civilian economy and technologies. The results are skewed priorities in all R&D undertakings.

The theory has been advanced that the military, having daily contact with advanced technology, being well organised and disciplined, has a specific role to play in economic development, modernisation and "nation-building" in third world societies. This became a kind of self-justification for military intervention and the setting of military priorities in national economies, including involvement in military R&D. Yet such a theory of the "modernising soldier" is highly flawed. Experience has shown, as stressed by Bhabani Sen Gupta of the New Delhi Jawaharlal Nehru University, that "not only has military rule failed to modernise and develop most of the third world countries, it has not even succeeded in holding off wars or insurrections."[74] Even where in the course of armaments investments some advance was achieved, "any positive result in spin-off or modernisation is either marginal or its narrow utility is tempered by its social and political implications."[75]

Third, once introduced in the arms producing countries of the Third World, military R&D becomes a vehicle for dependence on the flow of runaway military technologies, on spare parts, licenced production and maintenance support from the major powers.[76] Third world countries can rarely afford to compete in high technology with industralised countries, not to speak of costly investments in large-scale basic research which is the mainstay of R&D. By adopting the technological patterns of industralised countries, developing societies are buying alien system reproduction than real independence and expedient development. There is a close relationship between the choice of R&D, its thrust in science and technology and its socio-economic and political effects.[77] Indigenous and progressive models of economic advancement based on self-reliance and caring for ecological sustainability and democratic participation are being supplanted by military-influenced systems.

Several Western studies have indicated that defence investments have a positive effect on economic growth.[78] This may to some extent be true, especially in conditions when development is only at the starting point. But as the UN Study on *The Relationship Between Disarmament and Development* point out, the coexistence of military spending with economic growth, in some countries and in certain historical circumstances, does not necessarily provide evidence of a casual relationship between the two: it may rather reflect a process whereby military expenditures are squeezed out from the rate of growth.[79]

The most detailed studies on the economic spin-off effect from military R&D and armaments in third world countries have been carried out concerning India.

Saadet Deger of the Economic and Social Science Research Council at the Birbeck College, University of London, reports:

> It has been claimed that military-related R&D can be beneficial to the civilian sector. One of the less developed countries to be mentioned in this context is India. From the 1960s onwards, India has spent large sums of money on military R&D, as part of defence industralisation within an import-substituting strategy. Since self-sufficiency was the final objective, technological progress had to be generated endogenously, and R&D was considered the major vehicle of such

technical progress . . . Given the figures, there can be little doubt that military R&D is important in India. If the spin-off hypothesis is to be substantiated, India should receive the benefits of the substantial investment in defence inventions and research . . . Yet with all those factors loaded in favour of a beneficial effect, we find that the coefficients are insignificant and not much different from zero (in some cases they are actually negative). Thus in the apparently most favourable case, the effect of economic spin-off is negligible. Obviously, in other cases it could well be even less. We may conclude that the emphasis of spin-off in the defence literature is misplaced since its actual consequences are barely observable.[80]

Deger points to some basic reasons for the above outcome:

First the technology adopted by the defence sectors may be far too advanced . . . Secondly, strategic considerations would mean that the technology and research would be kept secret and would not be allowed to disseminate to civilian production. Thirdly, military projects are sometimes necessary for pure security reasons only and thus may not be able to generate high profits in commercial productions. Thus they may not be sufficiently cost-effective in a competitive market environment and so may be relatively useless for private enterpreneurs.[81]

The synergistic impact of the skewed global distribution of R&D reinforced by the inroads of military R&D in some third world countries has to be seen in the context of gross North-South inequalities in capital and scientific-technological skill. These uphold and deepen the polarisation in development and well-being between developed and developing countries. the outcome is intense socio-economic deprivation of a majority of the world population: 800 million people are living in absolute poverty, unable to meet minimal human needs; 770 million are not getting enough food for an active working life; 1 billion 300 million do not have safe water to drink; 100 million people have no shelter whatsoever; 14 million children die of hunger-related causes every year; 880 million adults cannot read and write.[82] Such socio-economic deprivation breeds anger, tension and conflict. It impinges on peace and war. More rational management of the vast world resources inherent in modern science and technology can make a fundamental difference for the human conditon. More than on any other grounds, peace stands today on the satisfaction of basic human needs.

5 Conclusion: science and technology for the betterment of the human condition

The current sharp acceleration of the race in science-based military technology has an ominous significance above and beyond the danger of war. It has a profoundly evil impact on the human condition. The working of military technology has produced a triple wickedness: it fuels and aggravates the course of the arms race, it deranges the economic performance of industralised countries, and it acts to sustain underdevelopment in the Third World — with all the implications this triple thrust has for the world economy and the maintenance of peace.

We urgently need a change of direction. Science and technology must once again heed their mission to civilisation: they should serve peace and not war; they should underpin disarmament and should work actively for the improvement of the human condition. Freeing science and technology from the malignant pursuit of means of destruction is a major universal human imperative.

It is thus of fundamental import that we devise measures to restrain military technology, so that we may move seriously to genuine disarmament and may buttress development.

This may be a tall order. But unless a start is made, we may find ourselves ever more forcibly in the grip of escalating armaments and an explosive developmental gap on the North-South divide.

With enough rationality and political will, we can check the technological momentum of the arms race by introducing qualitative-technological criteria into arms control and disarmament efforts.[83] But more than this is required: we need careful planning of a phased orderly redeployment of resources from military R&D and armaments, and their conversion for civilian use.[84] Further, we have to try to activate the large community of scientists and engineers currently employed in military R&D to resist their engagement in this domain on ethical and moral grounds. With conversion planning on the way, they should find satisfactory alternative employment in civilian R&D. Most of all, we have to make the workings of military R&D and its consequences more transparent, so as to mobilise public opinion. Thus we need to back the call to transcend the military technological compulsion and to make science and technology serve the common good of mankind.

Notes and References

1. *UNESCO Statistical Yearbook 1985*, introduction to chapter 5 'Science and Technology', p. V-1.
2. Some incongruencies may especially arise because of the use of various definitions for personnel under the category of R&D scientists and engineers, the conversion problem of non-convertible currencies, and the exact domain of expenditure. Thus, for instance, in the case of the Soviet Union the reference is to "scientific worker" and "expenditure on science". It appears then that while in 1980 the USSR had 36.6 per cent of the world R&D scientists and engineers, it spent on R&D only 15.6 per cent of global expenditure. At the same time North America with 18.0 per cent of global R&D scientists and engineers spent 32.1 per cent of world R&D expenditure. Some explanation of the above may be

found in the fact that US R&D is more capital-intensive. This may, however, not be fully satisfactory.

Another aspect of the definition of manpower employed in R&D is that if one adds technicians who received special scientific or technological training of at least three years after secondary education, the figure of R&D personnel increases sharply; for instance in the case of the USA by 40 per cent, of the Federal Republic of Germany and the UK by 100 per cent and in the case of France even by 200 per cent (see table 5.16).

3. Computed from *UNESCO Statistical Yearbook 1985*, tables 1.1, 5.1 and 5.2.
4. Soviet secrecy on armaments and military R&D expenditures should be of special concern. If the Soviet Union is serious with disarmament and development, as it persistently claims, it should be interested and helpful in making the armaments machine more transparent by revealing its dimensions and mode of operation. One should hope that Secretary-General Gorbachev's promise, in his message to the 1987 UN International conference on the Relationship Between Disarmament and Development, to reveal exact data on Soviet armaments in line with "glasnost and openness" so as "to come up to a realistic comparison of military budgets" will be put into effect.
5. Colin Norman, *The God That Limps: Science and Technology in the Eighties*, New York/London: W.W. Norton, 1981, p.72.
6. *Idem.*
7. *SIPRI Yearbook 1987 World Armaments and Disarmament.* Chapter 6, XII. 'Military research and development', London: Oxford University Press, 1987, p.153 (computations by Mary Acland-Hood).
8. UN Study Series 5, *The Relationship Between Disarmament and Development*, New York: United Nations, 1982, para 150.
9. *Idem.*
10. *Idem.*
11. *SIPRI Yearbook 1987, ibid.*
12. *Idem.*
13. Eugene Skolnikoff, "The Technological Factor Shaping East-West Relations", paper presented at the Sixth Annual Conference of the Institute for East-West Security Studies, Espoo, Finland, 11-13 June, 1987.
14. *Idem.*
15. *SIPRI Yearbook 1987.* pp. 153-154.
16. *SIPRI Yearbook 1974*, Stockholm: Almquist & Wicksell, 1974, p. 127.
17. See Rita Tullberg, " World Military Expenditures", in Marek Thee (Ed.), *Arms and Disarmament; SIPRI Findings*, Oxford/New York: Oxford University Press, 1986, p. 17.
18. *Ibid.*, chapter on "Military Research and Development" by Mary Acland-Hood, p. 29.
19. *Ibid.*, pp. 29-30.
20. *Idem.*
21. *Idem.*
22. *The Defense Monitor*, Vol XV, No. 3, 1986, p.3.
23. Mary Acland-Hood, "Military Research and Development", p. 29.
24. See Rita Tullberg, "World Military Expenditure," p. 18.
25. Cf. Michael Brzoska and Thomas Ohlson, *Arms Transfers to the Third World, 1971-1985*, SIPRI, Oxford/New York: Oxford University Press, 1987, chapter 1. "The flow of arms: main trends", pp. 1-14.
26. Cf. Leonard S. Spector, *Nuclear Proliferation Today*, A Carnegie Endowment Book, New York: Vintage Books, 1984. "Threshold countries" are generally considered to be India, Pakistan, South Africa, Israel, Argentina and Brazil. Aspiring to acquire nuclear weapons are also Iraq and Libya. See also Peter Lomas, "Attitudes of the nuclear threshold countries," in Josef Goldblat and

David Cox, *Nuclear Weapon Tests: Prohibition or Limitation?*, SIPRI and CIIPS, Oxford University Press, 1988, pp. 311-318.

27. Cf. Marek Thee, *Military Technology, Military Strategy and the Arms Race*, London: Croom Helm and New York: St. Martins Press, 1986; chapter 2: "Military Technology and Strategy after World War II; An overview", pp. 4-13.

28. Thomas B, Cochran, William M. Arkin, Milto M. Hoenig, *Nuclear Weapon Databook*, Vol. I. *US Nuclear Forces and Capabilities*, Cambridge, Mass.: Ballinger, 1984, p. 5.

29. T. B. Cochran, W. M. Arkin, R. S. Norris, M. M. Hoenig, *Nuclear Weapons Databook*, Vol. II. *US Nuclear Warhead Production*, Cambridge, Mass.: Ballinger, 1987, p. 5.

30. *Discriminate Deterrence*, Report of The Commission On Integrated Long-Term Strategy, January 1988, p.2 (no publisher mentioned).

31. *Ibid*. See also Ashton B. Carter, John D. Steinbrunner, Charles A. Zraket (Eds.) *Managing Nuclear Operations*, Washington, D.C.: The Brookings Institution, 1987; esp. chapter 17: Ashton B. Carter, "Assessing Command System Vulnerability," pp. 555-610.

32. Cf. Henry A. Kissinger, "the Future of NATO", *Washington Quarterly*, vol. 2, No. 4, Autumn 1979; and Spurgeon M. Keeny, Jr. and Wolfgng K. H. Panofsky, "Mad versus NUTS," *Foreign Affairs*, Vol. 60, No. 2, Winter 1981/82.

33. Cf. Frank Blackaby, "The Strategic Defense Initiative and Its Implications," in M. Thee (Ed.), *Arms and Disarmament: SIPRI Findings*, pp. 123-125.

34. Cf. the interview granted to NBC correspondent Tom Brokaw by Secretary-General Gorbachev on the eve of his visit to the United States, *Europa Archiv*, 43. H.Jahr, No. 1, 10.1.1988, p. D5.

35. See Bhupendra Jasani, "The military use of outer space," *SIPRI Yearbook 1986*, Oxford/New York: Oxford University Press, 1986, pp. 137-143.

36. See C. Kumar N. Patel and Nicolaas Bloembergen, "Strategic Defense and Directed Energy Weapons," *Scientific American*, September 1987, Vol. 257, No. 3;
    Douglas C. Walter and James T. Bruce, "SDI's Covert Reorientation," *Arms Control Today*, June 1987, Vol. 17, No. 5, pp. 2-8; and "A Physicist (Wolfgang Panofsky) Evaluates SDI," *Ibid.*, pp.26-29.

37. *Discriminate Deterrence*, pp. 1-3 and 21.

38. *Ibid.*, p. 49.

39. Joseph Fitchett, "New Missile Strategy Urged," *International Herald Tribune*, 11 January, 1988.

40. "A Frightening New Number Game," *US News & World Report*, 28 September, 1987.

41. Cf. Marek Thee, *Military Technology, Military Strategy and the Arms Race*, chapter "Greater Power Armaments Dynamics," pp. 101-126.

42. Cf. the circumstances of the decision to proceed from the production of the atomic bomb to the development of the hydrogen bomb, as reported in Herbert York, *The Advisors: Oppenheimer, Teller and the Superbomb*, San Francisco: Freeman and Col, 1976, p. 11.

43. On the origins of SDI see Frank Blackaby, "The Strategic Defense Initiative and Its Implications," pp. 123-124.

44. Cf. Hugh E. DeWitt, "Labs drive the arms race," *Bulletin of the Atomic Scientists*, Vol. 40, No. 9, November 1984; and Josephine Anne Stein and Frank von Hippel, "Laboratories versus a Nuclear Ban," *The New York Times*, 28 March, 1986.

45. W. K. H. Panofsky, "Science, Technology and the Arms Build-Up," paper presented at the Colloque Science et Désarmement, Insitute Français des Relations Internationales, Paris, 15-17 January, 1981.

46. Anatol Rapoport, "Conflict Escalation and Conflict Dynamics," in Raimo
    Värynen, Dieter Senghaas and Christian Schmidt (Eds.), *The Quest for Peace*,
    Sage Publications, 1987, pp. 176-177.
47. Cf. Robert McNamara and Hans A. Bethe, "Reducing the Risk of Nuclear
    War," *Bulletin of Peace Proposals*, Vol. 17, No. 2, 1986, p. 127.
48. See Richard K. Bets (Ed.), *Cruise Missiles: Technology, Strategy, Politics*,
    Washington D.C.: The Brookings Institution, p. 1; and
    Herbert York, *The Origins of MIRV*, Stockholm International Peace Research
    Institute, Report No. 9, August 1973, p.23.
49. UN Study Series 5, *The Relationship Between Disarmament and Development*,
    para 146.
50. See Seymore Melman, "Problems of Conversion from Military to Civilian
    Economy," *Bulletin of Peace Proposals*, Vol. 16, No. 1, 1985.
51. John Tirman (Ed.), *The Militarisation of High Technology*, Cambridge, Mass.:
    Ballinger, 1984, p.216.
52. Vassily Leontief, "New Technological Revolution — New International
    Outlook," paper presented at the Sixth Annual Conference of the Institute for
    East-West Security Studies, Espoo (Finland), 11-13 June, 1987.
53. *Idem.*
54. Lloyd J. Dumas, "Disarmament and Economy in Advanced Industrialised
    Countries — The US and the USSR," *Bulletin of Peace Proposals*, Vol. 12, No.
    1, 1981, p. 1.
55. Cf. Ruth Leger Sivard, *World Military and Social Expenditure 1985*,
    Washington, D.C.: World Priorities, pp. 35-36.
56. Lloyd J. Dumas, "University Research, Industrial Innovation and the
    Pentagon," in John Tirmar (Ed.), *The Militarisation of High Technology*,
    p.148. Cf. also Lloyd J. Dumas, *The Overburdened Economy*, Berkley/ Los
    Angeles/London: University of California Press, 1986, pp. 208-217.
57. "Will the US Stay Number One," *US News & World Report*, 2 February, 1987,
    p.20.
58. John Tirman (Ed.), *The Militarisation of High Technology*, p. 217.
59. *Ibid.*, pp. 215-221.
60. *SIPRI Yearbook 1987*, p. 158.
61. Cf. Mary Kaldor, *The Baroque Arsenal*, New York: Hill and Wang, 1981, pp.
    88-89.
62. Jim Stuart, "Critics of the Pentagon Challenge Value of 'Spinoff'
    Research,"*Atlanta Constitution*, 4 April, 1985.
63. Cr. Harvey Brooks, "The Impact of Military R&D and Spending on US
    Economy," 30 April, 1987 (memo to the American Academy of Arts and
    Sciences at Cambridge, Mass.).
64. Quoted in Lloyd J. Dumas, *The Overburdened Economy*, p.214.
65. Robert L. Park, "Superconductivity: The Contest Should Be Civilian and
    Open," *International Herald Tribune*, 6 August, 1987.
66. Cf. Mario Pianta, "High Technology Programmes: For the Military or for the
    Economy," *Bulletin of Peace Proposals*, Vol. 19, No. 1, 1988, pp. 68-70.
67. Jim Stuart, "Critics of the Pentagon Challenge Value of 'spinoff' Research."
68. Ruth Leger Sivard, *World Military and Social Expenditures 1987-88*, p. 42.
69. See Klaus Jürgen Gantzel and Jörg Meyer-Stamer (Eds.), *Die Kriege nach dem
    Zweiten Weltkrieg bis 1984, Daten und Analysen*, Munich/Cologne/London:
    Weltform Verlag, 1986, p. 140.
70. Ruth Leger Sivard, *World Military and Social Expenditures 1987-88*, p. 42.
71. *Idem.*
72. Rita Tullberg, "Military-Related Debt in Non-Oil Developing Countries, 1972-
    1982," in Marek Thee (Ed.), *Arms and Disarmament: SIPRI Findings*, p. 50.
73. Nigel Cross, "A Continent Starved of Science", *New Scientist*, No. 1565, 18

June, 1987, p. 34.

74. Bhabani Sen Gupta, "The Modernising Soldier: End of a Myth," *Bulletin of Peace Proposals*, vol. 10, No. 3, 1979, p. 273.

75. *The Relationship Between Disarmament and Development*, para 219a; see also Nicole Ball, "Military Expenditure and Socio-Economic Development," *International Social Science Journal*, Vol. 33, No. 1, 1983.

76. Cf. Giri Deshingkar, "Military Technology and the Quest for Self-Reliance: India and China," *International Social Science Journal*, Vol. 35, No. 1, 1983; see also *The Relationship Between Disarmament and Development*, para 219 c & f.

77. Cf. Soedjatmoko, "Political Systems and Development in the Third World," *Alternatives*, Vol. 8, No. 4, Spring 1983, pp. 491-492.

78. Cf. Saadet Deger, *Military Expenditure in the Third World Countries, The Economic Effects*, London/Boston and Henley: Routledge & Kegan Paul, 1986, p. 172.

79. Cf. *The Relationship Between Disarmament and Development*, para 182.

80. Saadet Deger, *op.cit.*, pp. 172-175.

81. *Ibid.*, p. 176.

82. Ruth Leger Sivard, *World Military and Social Expenditures 1987-88*, p. 25.

83. Cf. Mary Acland-Hood, "Restraining the Qualitative Arms Race"; and Marek Thee, "Military Technology, the Arms Race and Arms Control," in M. Thee (Ed.) *Arms and Disarmament: SIPRI Findings*, pp. 427-441; see also Marek Thee, "The Pursuit of a Comprehensive Nuclear Test Ban," *Journal of Peace Research*, Vol. 24, No. 1, 1988.

84. Cf. Lloyd J. Dumas, "Economic Conversion: the Crucial Link." (and following papers on the strategy of economy conversion) in *Bulletin of Peace Proposals*, Vol. 19, No. 1, 1988; see also Marek Thee, "UNO-Fonds "Abrustung und Entwicklung", *Dialog*, Heft 11, No. 1/1988 (PRIO English version: The Relationship Between Disarmament and Development: The Case of the International Disarmament Fund for Development").

8: A Step in the Right Direction

Andre Gunder Frank

We are on the brink of an abyss. Let's take a bold step forward. Unfortunately, this oft heard mad advice is more than a cruel joke. Instead Mikhail Gorbachev's letter to the United Nations on "The Reality and Guarantees of a Secure World" is a sane step back in the right direction.

Gorbachev analyzes the growing East West, North South and other conflicts and dangers in the world and proposes to strengthen the United Nations (UN) to deal with them. At first sight this proposals might appear (or be) an illusiory solution to the real problems that himself well analyzes. How could the UN do any more than reflect rather than resolve the conflicts among, not to mention within, its member states?

The answer must be sought in changing real world forces and political institutions, which underlie Gorbachev's analysis and proposal. In essence, the increasing international conflicts reflect the growth of the very multipolarity in the world in whose image the UN was founded at war's end. At that time however ironically, this multipolarity did not exist; because the United States exercised virtually undisputed hegemonic power in the world and in the UN. The United States has now lost this power, and the world has changed (back) in the direction of (interwar) kind for which the UN was originally designed as a conflict resolution agency. So why not adapt the UN to this new (old) reality and strengthen it to do better than its forerunner League of Nations? That is the Gorbachev proposal translated into plain English. As a step back in the right direction, it may not be so illusory and may be at least worth a try. Besides, who has a better idea?

Gorbachev writes of the mutual search for a balance of different, contradictory, yet real, interests of the contemporary community of states and nations...[which] has ceased to be a sphere which the big and strong divided into domains and zones of 'vital interests'. If domination by the big has ceased, it is not out of the goodness of the big heart(s), but because other powers have become strong to throw their real contradictory interests into the balance as well. Thus the USSR itself now counter balances US military power, Japan and Germany or the EEC counterbalance US economic power, and Third World non aligned countries counterbalance some of all of their, but especially US, political power in the UN and elsewhere. All have real economic, political, strategic, and other interests, which contradict each other and those in and of the US. Some of these are reflected in the UN.

Gorbachev expands his "balance of power" analysis more explicitly to include the third world countries in his book *Perestroika*. He points out repeatedly that the world is no longer as it was in 1947, when Churchill and Truman (he does not mention Stalin) divided it in two along the iron curtain. Today, "the time is ripe for abandoning views on foreign policy which are influenced by an imperial standpoint. Neither the Soviet Union nor the United States is able to force its will on others" (p.138).

In the age of nuclear bombs and terrorism (about which Gorbachev also makes concerned proposals), "the new political outlook calls for recognition of one more simple axiom: security is indivisible. It is either equal security for all or none at all" (p.142). However, can this security for all "proceed exclusively from the interests of, say, the Soviet Union or the United States, Britain or Japan? No! A balance of interests is needed. For the time being, no such balance exists. For now the rich get richer and the poor get poorer. Processes which could shake the entire system of international relations are, however, taking place in the Third World" (p.136). These include wars, about which unconcern is immoral, he says.

Therefore, Gorbachev also excludes earlier and contemporary variants of balance of power limited to the few: "Everything was a great deal simpler many years ago. There existed several powers which determined their interests and balanced them if they so managed, and warred it they failed" (p.135). Today, "by all indications, the West would like to keep things in the family, so to speak, with the Sevens, the Fives, and the like. This probably explains the attempts to discredit the United Nations" (p.140). However, "it seems obvious that every group of states and every country has interests of its own. From the view point of elementary logic, all these interests should find a reasonable reflection in world politics" (p.136). "The United Nations is the most appropriate forum for seeking a balance of interests of states, which is essential for the stability of the world" (p.140)

Why not, as Gorbachev proposes, let more of these conflicting interests be reflected if not resolved through the UN and its institutions and agencies? From the American conservatives' point of view precisely because the UN is becoming a more kaleidoscopic mirror of other interests and views rather than the docile instrument of American hegemonic foreign policy it once was — and that is why they want to pull the United States out of an organisation, which no longer operates predominantly in the American "national interest". Paradoxically however, only the strengthening and activation of the United Nations really to exercise the functions of a multilateral sounding board and agency for conflict resolution could make it too costly for the US to pull out on pain of isolating itself from where (some of) the real action is. But that would mean placing more of the action — and actors — on the UN stage, not to avoid or eliminate conflicts of interest but to reflect them there for all the world to see and act upon them.

Of course, making the UN more responsive, responsible and active in representing and potentially resolving contradictory interests implies according greater influence in and through the UN to powerful interests that are now underrepresented. These would have to include the political and economic interests of Japan, West Germany, and perhaps some big third world countries. The International Monetary fund, the World Bank, the General Agreement on Tariffs and Trade (as a stand in for the stillborn triplet of the International Trade Organisation) and some UN Specialised Agencies would have to be institutionally and politically better tied into the UN representative and decision making to negotiate the conflicting economic interests they now express largely independently. At the same time, the Soviet Union itself, China and other socialist countries would have to join/be admitted as full members to these international economic institutions (at which some are only just beginning to solicit observer status). Of course, this would also give institutional political reflection to their renewed real participation in the international division of labour and its contradictory interests in the (capitalist) world economy.

These changes would signify world institutional recognition and reflection of the existence of variety in the first, second and third "worlds", which Gorbachev explicitly recognizes and welcomes. These changes would also, however, give world institutional recognition to the real nonexistence of socialist development alternatives for most of the first and third world countries in the old world order. Gorbachev, Deng Xiaoping, and their newly revised Communist Party programmes now explicitly recognise the fact and accept this world order, which they now seek rejoin more than to change. Gorbachev proposes also to convert the UN into a kaleidoscopic mirror of this world reality

Gorbachev's political/institutional proposals to activate and strengthen the UN merit consideration (and elaboration in directions here indicated in parentheses):

1. Internationalization under the UN of the Geneva Conference on Disarmament (including arms and arms control, also on arms trade by other developed and developing countries).
2. A special UN humanitarian development/disarmament fund (with friendly relations with Non-Governmental Organisations).
3. A strengthened UN environmental agency (with more power to prevent transnational ecological degradation).
4. Greater UN protection of human rights (reviving League of Nations Nansen Passes for innocent refugees and holding violators of human rights, especially (ex) heads of states, *personally* accountable for their crimes).
5. A UN information programme on cultural diversity and tolerance (with UNOvision satellite TV broadcasts and videos).
6. A UN World Space Organization (under which the proposed Soviet-US Mars mission could be taken multilaterally).
7. A UN tribunal on international terrorism (including state [sponsored] terrorism and state generation of the seeds of private terrorism).
8. Mandatory jurisdiction for the International Court (which would have to be vastly expanded in jurisdiction, staffing and other resources).
9. Geographically rotating meetings of the UN Security Council.
10. More special (problem) sessions of the UN General Assembly.
11. More support for the UN General Secretary.
12. A UN Consultative Council uniting the world's intellectual elite (but not of philosopher kings, see below).

This last Gorbachev proposal is reminiscent of, albeit more limited than, one by the President of the International Development Alternatives Foundation (IFDA), Marc Nerfin. He has proposed (in an IFDA Dossier and summarized in *Development Dialogue* 1987:1 cited here) a tricameral UN General Assembly with political Prince, economic Merchant, and popular Citizen chambers as a goal for 2025 (why not before?). The first would represent governments as now. The second would represent *and regulate* the economic powers, be they transitional, multinational, national or local, belonging to the private, state of social sectors. The third chamber would realize the UN Charter's opening words, which Nerfin recalls, were "we the *peoples* of the United *Nations*" (and not we the governments of the united states of the world). This citizens' chamber, with an equal number of women and men, would speak for the people and their many popular groupings and associations. In practice, many of its member representatives may turn out to be intellectuals or intelligentsia as in the Gorbachev proposal.

There is no good reason why intellectuals, however, should be only an "elite". They need not only represent themselves, but rather a kaleidoscope of popular ethnic, religious, cultural, social and, of course, also political diversity. In the Nerfin proposal, this (intellectual?) citizen chamber would, of course, be deliberative if not executive, instead only consultative as in the Gorbachev proposal.

Both writers wish to address their ideas not only to the governmental powers that be. Nerfin's "exercise should, on the contrary, not only be directed at, but carried out with, the social actors themselves" (p.184). Gorbachev opens his book with a note to the reader expressing in the first sentence "my desire to address directly the people of the USSR, the United States, indeed every country." He calls for a "dialogue about the future of our planet" on which "we — all mankind — are in the same boat, and we can sink or swim together" (p.146). His book and the UN proposals reviewed here are his contribution to the dialogue, says Gorbachev. Others of us, as in the present book, must make our contributions as social actors ourselves as well. In Gorbachev's word's, nothing will be done unless we act.

9: Global Greenhouse or Green World?

Luciana Castellina

Is it possible to revitalise the United Nations, which today faces a profound crisis? There are enormous global problems of environmental mess. This theme was considered by a UN seminar which prepared a working paper on the building of a "third generation" of international institutions to go beyond the limits inherited from the old League of Nations, and the present inhibitions of the UNO itself, to reach to a more appropriate institutional response to the problems of our own time.

If present trends continue, trends which indicate a very gradual but constant increase in earth temperatures, as a result of the "greenhouse effect", then, half-way into the coming century, in about sixty years' time, it will have become impossible to cultivate grain either in the mid-West of the United States, or in the Soviet Ukraine.

Within a century temperatures will have risen to a level sufficient to melt the polar ice-caps and submerge many coastal cities.

These events do not lie in a far future. They are by no means historically distant, but lie within the lifespans of our children or grandchildren.

These are things that we know: ecologists have been warning about them, with increasing alarm, for some time. But at the political level, reactions are evasive. This is natural, because political timetables run on a short fuse, between elections, or within the span of a particular leadership. If one wants consensus, one looks for it in the short run. It is impossible to obtain easy agreement to meet, today, costs which will present themselves in days long after the tenure of present administrations. Carl Sagan has tried a less tentative approach. In a recent seminar sponsored by *Parliamentarians for Global Action* (the group which launched and kept going the famous Five Continent Peace Appeal) he offered a plan. The seminar sought approaches to a system of global security, in an appropriate programme of political action. Sagan posed a provocative, but very realistic, question: "Let's look at the desertification of the mid-West, or of the Ukraine, and let's assume that the alarm will finally sound loudly enough to affect even those lobbies which are presently blocking the alternatives. Let's assume that even the USSR and the USA will join their forces to fight this calamity, and that in order to reach a solution they will go to China, which has the most enormous coal reserves on Earth, to warn her that the use of such reserves will produce catastrophe." "It is foreseeable" said Sagan, "that the Chinese might respond: 'We are sorry, but for us the effects are more bearable than for you, and you have already had your time. We shall go ahead, and good luck to you: it's your problem.'"

At this point, either the most advanced countries must be able to offer the Chinese possible alternatives (which are feasible, but not yet "convenient", if cost-benefit relations are calculated in the short-to-medium run) at prices low enough to dissuade the Chinese from using their coal, or they will be tempted to overrule such use by force.

The example here is China, but of course this reasoning is applicable to all of the Third World, which is still generating enough oxygen for us to breathe, because it remains "underdeveloped". So, the problem of common security starts from here. Immediately it calls us to face the need for a different way of regulating the world's affairs, of an international instrument which defends the interests of all that population without votes in today's elections, who are the peoples of the future.

Is it possible to revitalise the United Nations Organization to begin to cope effectively with such an agenda, which becomes more urgent all the time, and which needs a strong authority or government to meet it? This seems to be a naive question. People think of the UNO as a "dead dog". They tend to laugh about such pretensions. And yet the question is not so simplistic at all, and even at the political level people have started to worry at it.

Ecological devastation, the enormous accumulation of weaponry, and growing world confusion all witness the crumbling of an old order, and the open emergence of crisis. The old order was unequal, a bad order, but it was order of a kind, and therefore reassuring. Now it is passing, and with its going disquiet is growing.

The American press is full of these things, more than the European press. This was especially true after Gorbachev's long, and unexpected, article of September last, written for the UN General Assembly. Now the Soviet Union, which never used to prioritise this institution, is saying "be careful. Today's peoples have many fragmented interests, diversities, contradictions: nevertheless, we have arrived at the point where it is imperative to do some things in concert." More: today the Soviets are following these bold words with deeds.

The enormous backlog of Soviet debts to the UN, from the time of the Korean war onwards, has now been discharged. This legacy dates back to the time of the blue berets, in the early 'fifties, when the US dominated the UN Organization, before the inrush of all the third world's independent states to membership. Since then, things have changed, but the glass palace has remained little more than a stage for proclamations, without practical results. World affairs have been managed, in so far as they have been managed at all, by the privileged interactions of the two superpowers.

The difference between the assumptions of this epoch and the writings of Gorbachev is manifest especially in the attempt to overcome the old bipolar block confrontation. Interest in this is widespread and electric. It is fuelled by the urge to escape from an ever-greater squeeze, which had been throttling all those caught between the powers.

The new line announces itself practically. No more red telephones between Moscow and Washington, but between the Secretary-General and all the Security Council States, plus the head of the Non-aligned Group of States; international organisms to collect information and scrutinise all conflict areas, in such a manner as to preclude unilateral interventions; the establishment of non-governmental commissons, on the model of the Brandt, Palme or Brundtland Commissions, in order to analyse the roots of conflict or disaster, and to evolve independent proposals for solutions; the immediate despatch of UN peace-keeping forces (not after the event), well-equipped, integrated in their own national forces, yet acting as part of a rapid-intervention international force, to intervene in emergencies in which countries are threated or attacked (from Afghanistan to Central America to Namibia, and naturally, to the Gulf); international tribunals on human rights and on the rights of the peoples, with jurisdictional powers.

Our seminar was looking for a viable project: in search of this it went through a variety of proposals before reaching agreement. The agreement reached was clear. We need to build a third generation of international institutions, which can transcend the limitations of the old League of Nations, but also go beyond the restrictions of the UN system and its five-power veto. The seminar also tackled the more difficult theme raised by New Zealand, concerning nuclear deterrence. If one considers nuclear deterrence is the foundation of present security policy, then such deterrence cannot remain a monopoly, but must be brought under collective control. This implies a minimum level of nuclear force, in the hands of, say, the United Nations.

Only this kind of project can offer general guarantees to everybody: because evidently the bomb cannot be disinvented, and even though one seeks to limit the size of arsenals, or transfer out to a reliance on conventional weapons instead of nuclear ones, the fatal discovery has been made, and is in reach wherever conflict threatens. The only real safeguard now possible is to place control of nuclear force in the hands of a genuinely multilateral organ, within a framework of accountability and legality. Such a framework would guarantee a truly multipolar order.

From this seminar as a foundation, the future campaigns of this strange network of Parliamentarians for Global Action [grouping more than 600 deputies from assemblies across the third world and throughout the globe] turn towards the transformation of the United Nations. Today this seems a futuristic aspiration. No reform of the UN will ever make it more effective until the other international institutions of the Bretton Woods postwar financial settlement remain subject to distinct and opposing, non-democratic, imperatives. In particular, it is obvious that conflicts of interest make it difficult to foresee a sufficient convergence to bring about reform. The crisis of the UN is rooted in a more profound disorder in the world economic system. It is also true that the national states are losing powers within this global crisis, which is undermining not only states, but the blocs into which they have aligned themselves. Everybody feels more vulnerable, more dependent on the mercies of others.

The renewed attention to the United Nations is thus a symptom of attitude changes which could become a new *common* sense: a new concept of security. Even if this takes time to evolve institutional embodiment, such a common sense would itself become a powerful sense.

10: A Third Generation

Joop den Uyl

During the 40th anniversary of the United Nations many discussions took place on reforming the UN system. This need for reform could be attributed to several causes.

● The UN is experiencing a financial crisis and needs to cut expenses.

● There is increasing criticism of the functioning of the UN system vis-à-vis the Charter objectives.

● There is a retreat from internationalism and multilateralism, the continuation of which can lead to a reduction of the role of the UN and even to a breakdown of the system.

● There is a feeling among people that the UN is outdated and not able to cope with the changes in society.

World organizations started in the middle of the 19th century. Compared with everything before, the UN constitutes an elaborate system of international co-operation. The League of Nations and the UN have been great steps forward in a history determined by the absolute sovereignty of nations, by imperialism and by an endless set of wars.

The development of modern arms — nuclear arms in particular — has increased the necessity of treaties and rules on a global scale. Some treaties between the superpowers, such as SALT and ABM, have shown to be of the highest importance in maintaining peace and preventing world destruction. However, such treaties, and those for maintaining outer space for peaceful purposes and for the exploration of the seabed, need to be integrated into worldwide arrangements to ensure adherence and implementation.

More inequality
Likewise, the technological revolution promises better living and working conditions but it also has the tendency to increase inequality within and between nations. Avoiding that danger demands common policies.

Preserving the environment from destruction necessitates worldwide common policies to limit and end the poisoning of the water, soil and air.

What we should think about is how we may organise our common interests as world citizens, so that we may enter the 21st century as a world community prepared to meet the above-mentioned challenges.

The world has changed considerably since the UN was founded 40 years ago. Then, there were about 50 nations; now it has 159 member states. Then, there were three billion people on earth, now five. Then, nuclear weapons were still to come; now they are an obsession for the whole world. Then, exploration of outer space was a dream; now military uses of outer space are an actual threat. Today the world has developed information and communication systems that were hardly conceivable 40 years ago.

New regional organisations have come into existence during the postwar period, largely as a result of the decolonisation process. And there are now about 350 organisations working on a global scale.

It is against this background that Maurice Bertrand, of the UN's Joint Inspection Unit, phrased his formula of "a third generation of world institutions".[1] After the League of Nations and the experience of the United Nations, we should think about the character and function of a third generation of united nations.

There is a minimalist and maximalist school of thinking. The minimalists, who seem to be strong in the US, are inclined to liken the UN to a private organisation, limiting its scope and working area. This view has been stimulated by the bipolar relationship between the superpowers which consider the UN as an instrument of third world countries to impose decisions upon them.

The maximalists try to build up a system in which ultimately the world is governed by one government with authorities and powers comparable with the national state.

What should be aimed at is a clear identification of the interests of humanity which should be ensured by a world organisation with law enforcement powers. As far as the present UN is based on a legally agreed transfer of power from national states to the world organisation, it is of a unique character. That element should be strengthened.

What contributes so much to the loss of authority of the present UN is the lack of enforcement of its resolutions. The European Court of Justice has to deal with an average of two cases a day; the International Court of Justice an average of about two a year. That makes all the difference between an organisation gaining and an organisation losing relevance. Reforming the UN has to mean increasing its relevance.

From the organisational point of view, the UN is chaotic, bureaucratic and burdened with a wrong type of decentralisation. The Secretariat administration is top-heavy, and the specialised agencies and subsidiary organisations have grown out of hand.

The General Assembly (GA) in 1985 charged a high-level group of experts to report on the administrative and managerial problems of the UN. The report,[2] which has 71 recommendations, is important and useful but it does not deal with the relationship between the Secretariat and the specialised agencies, nor with the problems of the division of tasks and the co-ordination of programmes and activities within the system, as they fell outside the group's mandate. The mandate of the group as given by the GA contributes to the misunderstanding that the problem of the UN is primarily a managerial one. That is wrong. The problem is a structural one.

When we say that the problem of the UN is a structural one, we mean that we have to find a structure that can better deal with the problems to be solved than the existing fragmented structure of a multitude of sectoral organisations. Is Bertrand's proposal to substitute the activities of a set of sectoral organisations with "regional development agencies or enterprises" the key to solving the UN problem?

To a certain degree that could be true; it should certainly be explored. Regionalisation had been proposed earlier in another context. In 1978 Jan Tinbergen[3] proposed to develop a world employment plan on the basis of comparative advantages of regions in the world.

A rebuilding of the existing UN agencies into regional agencies will succeed only if the region has a political identity. It is a major political challenge to create and stimulate these regional political identities. Certainly it will take many years to implement such an institutional reorganisation. But the nation state offers the example. No national government is thinkable without provinces, counties and local governments.

The great "malheur" of the UN has been that the great powers keep their fundamental negotiations outside the UN because they do not want to be subjected to the voting mechanism of 159 countries. The decision-making process in economic and financial affairs is notably done within the framework of the IMF with weighted voting.

Since 1974 the seven major industrialised countries meet annually at world summits, where policies are co-ordinated and decisions to be taken by ministers of finance or heads of central banks are prepared. The European Community, since 1973, also has summits of heads of state or government.

Compared with these mechanisms, the UN seems powerless and irrelevant. With the exception of speeches by ministers of foreign affairs at the beginning of the GA, the UN is the playground of ambassadors and officials.

Whoever wants to make the UN more relevant has to change this. That is to say, conditions have to be created which make it interesting and worthwhile for politically responsible ministers to influence decisions to be taken. The tragedy of the UN is that the greater its membership, the more rich nations have withdrawn from it.

An 'Economic United Nations'

Proposals for an "Economic United Nations" with an "Economic Security Council" are aimed at overcoming the present decay of the UN system. Certainly, the present machinery for co-ordination of economic, financial and social activities, mainly dependent on the ECOSOC, does not work sufficiently. That is mostly due to the fact that financial and economic decisions of major importance are taken outside the UN framework. But it is also because the UN lacks a long-term strategy for economic development.

Successive special GA sessions in 1974 and 1975 accepted the concept of a "new international economic order". This concept has never been worked out properly and insofar as it aimed at a transfer of power to the poor nations it has been neglected and ridiculed by richer nations from the very start. During the world economic crisis at the beginning of the 1980s the attempt at global negotiations broke down.

Thus there is a clear need to create machinery for financial and economic decision-making at a global scale. But it would be a mistake to think that an economic UN could be simply formed alongside a "political" UN.

What is needed at the world level is the integration of political and economic decision-making. In such a process the smaller countries should accept that in the process of integrated financial and economic policies, some weighted voting is acceptable. The stronger economic nations should in turn accept that in those economic and financial decisions, the poor nations should have a real vote. Such a reform could pave the way to a virtual integration of the IMF and the World Bank into the UN system.

The existing structure of the UN to maintain peace should also be reformed. Great care should be taken, however, not to damage the achievements in the sphere of peacekeeping operations.

Limitation of the veto power is at best thinkable at the end of a process of reform of the functioning of the UN, not at the beginning.

But there are quite a few changes which could be applied to the existing mechanism. One is to strengthen the preventive task of the Secretary-General. Another is the possibility that the veto-wielding powers together accept a specific responsibility for peacekeeping between third world countries.

It cannot be denied that part of the problem with the peacekeeping function of the UN is connected with the growth in its membership. The estrangement of the US from the UN system depends to a certain degree on the frustration about the "one country, one vote" principle in an organisation with 159 members, so different in size and financial contributions.

How then should reform be organised? First, the ongoing implementation of the recommendations of the 1986 High-Level Group. Second, a careful study of the inter-governmental structure in the economic and social fields to be concluded with dispatch. Third, creation of an independent group of eminent persons to report on the present and future functions and structure of the UN as a co-ordinating world organisation.

Another proposal is to have a small group work on the role of the UN for five years under supervision of a group of experts.

Organisations are instruments to reach goals. At present, we have reached too little. Notwithstanding the UN and hundreds of other organisations, the arms race has gone on, hunger has not disappeared, inequality within and between nations has grown and we are endangering the environment and in the process the fate of future generations.

Footnotes
1. *Some reflections on reform of the United Nations*, Maurice Bertrand, December 1985.
2. *Report of the Group of High-Level Intergovernmental Experts to Review the Efficiency of the Administrative and Financial Functioning of the United Nations*, August 1986.
3. *A World Employment Plan*, Tinbergen, Den Uyl, Pronk en Kok, 1978.

11: Reforming the United Nations

Ken Coates

The only universal organization in today's world is the United Nations. Fifty-one states joined forces to found it in 1945, and year after a year it has subsequently grown to its present membership of 159 states. This process of growth has reflected the erosion of the great European empires, and the success of the many movements for national independence in Africa, Asia, and Latin America. All this is a great achievement of mankind, and needs to be vigorously defended against its powerful detractors.

However, the United Nations General Assembly consists of diplomatic representatives of states, each of which carries one vote, regardless of the size of the population it may represent. During the earliest years of the UN, there were frequent discussions about the establishment of a directly elected Chamber for the Organization. Naturally, such a proposal raises great difficulties for the principle of national sovereignty, which was written into the founding principles of the new organization. The first of these insists on "The sovereign equality of all . . . members". The last of them renders this specific by insisting that "nothing in the Charter is to authorize the United Nations to intervene in matters which are essentially within the domestic jurisdiction of any state".

When the League of Nations had been established, following the First World War, it constituted a response to a whole generation of pacifist and socialist advocates who had sought to establish conditions in which national interests might be arbitrated by a supra-national influence. Thus, during the war itself, which he consistently opposed, Bertrand Russell wrote:

> "If civilization is to continue, Europe must find a cure for this universal reign of fear with its consequence of mutual butchery. One way in which it might be cured is that the civilized nations, realising the horror and madness of war, should so organize themselves as to make it practically certain that no advantage can be gained by initiating an attack. For this purpose it would be necessary to avoid exclusive alliances and to form a

League of Peace, which should undertake, in the event of a dispute, to offer mediation, and, if one party accepted mediation while the other refused it, to throw the whole of its armed support on the side of the party accepting mediation, while, if both parties refused mediation, the League should throw its weight against whichever party proved to be the aggressor."[1]

To this prescription was joined a denunciation of secret diplomacy and other ills which were associated with the outbreak of the 1914 conflict. The English historian A.J.P. Taylor, summarized all this very clearly:

"Bertrand Russell provides a striking example. The final chapter of *The Foreign Policy of the Entente* laid down Radical principles of foreign policy: no annexations: renunciation of the right of capture; universal arbitration; no alliances or understandings; 'we shall not engage in war except when we are attacked.' Appended to this is a footnote: 'Unless a League of Great Powers could be formed to resist aggression everywhere . . . In that case, we might be willing to participate in a war to enforce its decisions.'"[2]

Taylor mercilessly captures the contradiction in this commitment:

"Woodrow Wilson himself did much the same, when he thought to change the character of the treaty of Versailles by tying the Covenant of the League to its coat-tails. Every advocate of the League weighed with two measures. Their books described at length the misdeeds of statesmen all over the world. Then, in a short final chapter, they assumed that the same statesmen would become persistently virtuous once a League of Nations had been set up."

This contradictory position was still continued after 1945, even if the disintegration, over some decades, of colonial empires, and the rise of non-alignment, offered hopes that things might improve. In the absence of higher authority, governments would usually exercise their sovereignty to defend their narrow interests. Some of the lessons of the weakness of the League of Nations were drawn by the architects of the UN. Thus the charter of the International Court of Justice was deliberately incorporated into the Charter of the UN itself.[3]

Resonant declarations accompanied the promulgation of the United Nations Charter in San Francisco during the summer of 1945. Speaking in a foreign affairs debate in the British Parliament, shortly after the election of the 1945 Labour Government, Anthony Eden, the Conservative spokesman, opened with one of these:

"We have somehow to take the sting out of nationalism. We cannot hope to do this at once. But we ought to start working for it now, and that, I submit, should be the first duty of the United Nations ... I want to go to a world where the relations between nations can be transformed in a given period of time, as the relations between England, Scotland and Wales have been transformed."[4]

Such a transformation clearly implied intrusions into the principles of national sovereignty, as generations of Scottish and Welsh nationalists will readily testify. Bevin had to respond for the first time in his new role as Foreign Secretary in the Attlee administration. In what one of his biographers has called the "greatest speech of his life"[5] he went far beyond Eden to embrace Taylor's criticism of the arguments which Russell had espoused three decades earlier.

"We are driven relentlessly to the necessity of a new study for the purpose of creating a world assembly, elected directly from the peoples to whom the governments that formed the United Nations are responsible, to make a world law which the people will accept, and be morally bound to carry out . . .

The common man is the great protection against war, and the supreme act of government is, after all, the horrible duty of deciding matters which affect the life and death of the people. That rests on the House of Commons as far as this country is concerned.

I would merge that power into the greater power of a directly elected world assembly in order that the great repositories of destruction and science, on the one side, might be their property, to protect us against their use, and, on the other hand, it could easily determine whether a country was going to act as an aggressor or not.

I am willing to sit with any body, any party, or any nation to try to devise a franchise or a constitution for a world assembly for a limited objective — the objective of peace."[6]

In spite of his enthusiasm for this utopian project, Bevin was soon to prove himself very much more agnostic about the actually existing organization of United Nations. His main biographer, Lord Bullock, chronicles a whole series of events in which Bevin showed himself keen to prefer national, and indeed imperial, interests over global ones.[7]

But the argument for an elected world assembly continued to develop. In 1953, two American lawyers, Grenville Clark and Lewis B. John, of the Harvard Law School, published a project on *Peace through Disarmament and Charter Revision*.[8] They proposed a detailed solution to Bevin's constitutional problem. Each member state of the United Nations would be entitled to one representative for each five million of its electors, or major part thereof. There would be an upper limit of thirty representatives from any one state. States with less than two and a half million citizens would be represented by delegates with voice but no vote. Adjustments would be made as populations changed, within a maximum global representation of four hundred deputies.

Other proposals for a bicameral governing body, maintaining the existing General Assembly and adding a parallel Popular Assembly, were advanced by World Federalists and the World Association of Parliamentarians for World Government. From the University of Chicago came a proposal for continental electoral colleges to appoint members of a global parliament. This debate continued in a fairly lively state throughout the first postwar decade.[9]

But during all this time, the UN was falling far short of the status of universality. Numerous nations were excluded from membership. The most towering example of these was People's China, barred in 1949 and kept at bay until 1971. As the cold war raged, and nuclear weapons proliferated horizontally (somewhat) and vertically (a great deal), so the consolidation of blocs progressively stifled the striving for direct international popular representation.

The detonation of the first thermonuclear device provoked worldwide concern, and following the Russell-Einstein Appeal, directly engendered first the Pugwash Movement of scientists, and later a new popular movement for nuclear disarmament. Addressing this, Russell returned, in two books, to his old theme of world government.[10] Now, he sought a world legislature with the sole power to register and confirm treaties, and revise them if they conflicted with international law. This body would be able to object to "violently nationalist systems of education" if they appeared to constitute a danger to peace. It would sustain an executive with control of armed forces, of which it would hold a monopoly. And it would confer on the institutions of international law "the same authority as belongs to national courts".[11] In an early essay on the same theme, he advocated a transitional approach through conciliation to an international authority.[12] It is fair to say that these proposals attracted less serious attention than any of Russell's other arguments about the nuclear peril, developed at the same time, and indeed, in the same writings. Reform of the United Nations has never entirely disappeared from the agenda of political discourse, but it is difficult to deny that it has long ceased to attract widespread attention, or any degree of priority in public opinion.

Nonetheless, global integration was continuing, and rapidly continuing, by other means. The acceleration of colonial freedom movements continued in spite of frontal imperial interventions by the European powers and both overt and covert destabilisation by the American Central Intelligence Agency. Non-alignment became a power in the world. The doors of the United Nations could not remain for ever locked against this vast upheaval in the global system, and the organisation became, by the beginning of the present decade, almost universally inclusive. It also began to make decisions which were unwelcome to authority in the most potent chancelleries of the world.

At the same time, great political and economic changes were under way. There were always many obstacles to the surrender of national sovereignty to any supranational power, be it never so carefully conceived. Some of these obstacles reflected particular interests, and were shabby and sometimes exploitative. But perhaps the most important obstacle of all was not at all concerned with vested interests. It drew its force from the fact that it reflected progressive concerns and commanded support from all who were likely to listen to internationalist appeals. It was, of course, the fact that the conquest of democracy had either taken place at the national, state level, or not at all. Democratic power, in the postwar world, was national power, and therefore sovereignty was not merely linked with particular national interests, but also with a universal political aspiration, above all in the working populations, and among the most progressive political parties. Democratic power grew in the more economically developed countries with the establishment of the Keynesian world order, within whose framework prospered national economic management, regulation of demand, full employment, and strong, if usually subordinate, trade unions. In all such countries there arose a consensus of welfare and political balance. But the same economic order provided ideal soil for the growth of transnational corporations, within whose massive concentrations were gathered more and more of the world's production and trade, and ultimately the very real capacity to evade or nullify national state policies on the development of their economies.

National democracies, in short, soon began to face the pressures of an international economy, completely beyond their direct control. The world of the transnationals abrogated the age of Keynes, and confronted national governments with stark choices, all of which were increasingly incompatible with the postwar democratic balances. The same violent focusing of economic power burnt out even more damaging holes in the social fabric of the emergent nations, and engendered strong support for the call for a new international economic order.

But, however comprehensive the membership of the United Nations, its powers were nowhere near adequate to meet such a challenge. Indeed, the UN agencies most directly affected came under sustained criticism and attack. In the United States, a sinister organization called the Heritage Foundation spent vast sums of money on campaigns against such bodies as UNESCO and the

FAO, as well as funding onslaughts on the UN system as a whole. The Americans and some of their clients abandoned UNESCO. First the French and then the United States decided to ignore and then defy the International Court of Justice. Indeed, the wider the representativity of the UN, the more recalcitrant has been the conduct of international relations by the United States Government. In 1985 this conduct provoked strong admonitions from the Socialist International.

"For much of the post-war period, many countries saw the United States as combining both might and right, with the moral authority of administrations identified with the New Deal, Lend Lease, the fight against fascism, Marshall Aid and the establishment of the United Nations. Today, the United States is identified, by many countries, with Vietnam, the invasion of Grenada, support for Pinochet's Chile, political leverage on aid, and nuclear proliferation.

Over the last seven years, the United States has not agreed to any outcome of North-South negotiations, whether the Common Fund, new or renewed commodity agreements, the Law of the Sea Convention, or a new round of global negotiations. Recently, it has not only withdrawn from UNESCO but has also refused to recognize International Court of Justice verdicts on Central America, refused to agree a minimally adequate replenishment of IDA funds, and has attempted to relegate IFAD to virtual insignificance.

Lately, the US has also made known that it is going for 'a firmer, more forthright and less patronizing attitude in negotiating with developing countries', that it will no longer 'reward the radical and non-serious elements of international organizations by accepting their proposals as bases for negotiation', and that it will sometimes refuse to negotiate, or will abstain from negotiations altogether. The US and other critics may be right in claiming that improvements in the character and format of these North-South negotiations are necessary. But to plead for improvements is one thing. It is another to threaten with non-participation before negotiations even start.

The result has been not only US unwillingness to agree to recovery programmes, reform of institutions or redistribution towards the poorest countries. It has also increasingly meant a rejection by the United States of multilateral institutions, save on its own terms, for its own purposes. The message has not gone unnoted."

In 1987, the United Nations lives in a world which may, hopefully, be about to enter on the first tentative steps to nuclear disarmament. But however great the will to peace, the obstacles to that peace do not consist in arms alone, but rather in the conditions which promote the accumulation and use of arms. And what are these conditions? There is a worldwide crisis of indebtedness, in which whole families of nations find that their investment potential has been confiscated for years ahead. Structural problems of great severity afflict most 'advanced' economies even during times of relative upturn. Almost 20 million people lack work in Europe. Recovery of full employment is far from the top of the agendas of those governments which have departed most considerably from it. If the United States goes ahead with plans to balance its budget which have already been mooted, European unemployment will rise again to some 24 million. The effects in the South will be catastrophic. Development in the South, and recovery in large areas of the North, certainly call for international co-operation in new ways, and offer the United Nations and its agencies much scope for action.

And yet the crisis of recovery and development remains a crisis of nation states, of national democracy, and of sovereignty. Unemployed people in Spain or the Netherlands want jobs in Spain and the Netherlands, not some abstract upturn which passes over their heads. The political impasse of the present crisis does not result from too much national sovereignty, but too little. National democracy has by no means been overtaken by accessions of powers to the UN, but bypassed and neutralised by arbitrary and unaccountable private economic powers. The most rigorous conservatives in Europe seek to solve the resultant problems, not by democratic advance in international co-operation, but by reverting to pre-democratic forms of laissez-faire, at any rate concerning the most potent corporations, actually abrogating or repealing those democratic powers which might be conceived to impede corporate aggrandisement.

In this painful world it is plain that democracy cannot simply jump over the states in which it has been confined. It is bound to seek to defend its national spaces, and to recover control over powers which have been filched from it. Today is not the day when democrats can afford to join in the lobby to annul rights which are proving all too difficult to preserve: and yet international co-operation, joint action between states and democratic agencies, becomes, increasingly, a prior condition for even the most limited success in the struggle against unbridled economic concentration.

Because such co-operation is not easy it will be likely to emerge tentatively, and to be cautious in its initial scope. And because the development of the United Nations itself will be determined in this process, we must face up, at the same time, to two contradictory imperatives.

One: national independence and autonomy must be upheld as still the most basic area of democratic advance.

Two: the growth of transnational economic power, and the weight of accompanying crisis, demand measures of international co-ordination which can best be undertaken within a democratic framework.

The first principle of this argument is of course linked to the second. The national interests, and the democracy of Nicaragua or French Polynesia, for instance, would be well served by acts making International Court judgments enforceable. The linkage works also in reverse, however, because the resistance of those powers found culpable in such actions as these spills over to inhibit their co-operation even in areas in which their own interests might obviously benefit.

All these considerations may combine to persuade us that the time is not yet propitious for us to tackle the agenda set up by Russell, or by Bevin in his headier moods. States will think it ill-advised to surrender still more of that competence they precariously retain, constantly eroding as it is in an unfriendly economic environment. On the contrary, they will be likely to seek, in their international actions, to recover power and sovereignty, and to regenerate democratic influence, precisely in order to address their domestic crises more effectively.

Yet the existence of a universal international forum is too precious an asset to be ignored in this process. There is a stronger case than ever before for direct elections to a United Nations popular assembly, provided we pitch it at the right level, addressing the problems involved in it realistically, and aiming for as much as will be seen to be useful at the present juncture.

What functions should be addressed in such a case? The answer seems very plain. It is at the level of world public opinion formation that the present United Nations system is weakest. Widespread international action can be mobilised on specific issues, such as opposition to apartheid, or relief of famine: but the movements engaged in these causes usually emerge spontaneously, without directly impinging on the United Nations until they have already become strong; while there remain numerous urgent questions about which even informed pressure groups within different countries act in isolation, without forming the very linkages which could be decisive in the presentation of their arguments. If there were a UN popular consultative assembly, it would perform major services even were it to exercise no physical powers whatever. First, supposing in the modern age that every six million adults in the world were to be invited to choose a representative for such a world forum, this could imply a process of election in which all the key issues would be extensively discussed. Parties would gell to express the different options, and many concealed issues would be opened up. The press and television services would shift their attention, for a vital if brief period, to a global agenda. Second, national democratic forces would quickly discover their most appropriate international partners in dialogue and joint action. Linkages would emerge quickly and by rational choice rather than haphazardly and in the light of restricted and sometimes false information. Thirdly, the received perceptions of national interest would face both internal and external scrutiny. Fourthly, even the most limited assembly would become a focus for a thousand lobbies and causes, and a sounding board for all the innumerable non-governmental agencies. Lastly, by expanding the concern of the peoples for the United Nations, we would ensure that all the reactionary and fissiparous lobbies against it would receive a decisive rebuff.

Of course, such a consultative body could be constituted with no power, little power, or somewhat more. Beginning with a procedure in which conventions might be adopted to express the majority view, it might follow the example of the International Labour Organization, and monitor and encourage ratification and enforcement of such conventions by responsible governments. Moving further, it might exercise a range of influences within the specialised agencies. At a higher level, it might begin to discharge some of the functions which used to be argued by reformers in the 'fifties, such as monitoring the enforcement of treaties. But the advance we should seek should be evaluated not in terms of power, but in terms of influence and the expression of opinion. Nobody should underestimate the force of a global forum, even if it chooses to move forward slowly, respecting national differences, and seeking no more than the opportunity to persuade the sovereign states of the world of certain universal priorities.

Is it conceivable that the separate states might see merit in such an arrangement? Can we not set about designing a global framework of democratic opinion-formation which can underpin and reinforce the rights of nations to determine their own development? Can we, indeed, continue to develop our separate national democracies in the difficult environment of world-wide corporations and high technologies, *without* some such general international framework? The peace movement has coined a useful slogan: "think globally, act locally". Will this not be far more susceptible of implementation when there exists a truly global democratic forum?

In spite of the long disputes in the development of such a popular world assembly, these questions seem once again to be relevant at a time of general crisis, which is, perhaps, also a time of new hope.

Footnotes
1. *War: The Offspring of Fear* reproduced in Stansky: *The Left and the War.* NY OUP 1969 pp.111-2
2. A.J.P. Taylor: *The Trouble-makers — Dissent over Foreign Policy.* Hamish Hamilton, 1958, pp.132-5.
3. UN Charter, Chapter XIV, Articles 92-96.
4. Cited in J.T. Murphy *Labour's Big Three.* Bodley Head, 1948, p.234.

5. *Ibid.*
6. *Ibid,* p.235
7. A. Bullock: *Ernest Bevin — Foreign Secretary 1945-51:* Vol. 3 of the *Life of Ernest Bevin*, Heinemann 1983.
8. See also the same author: *World Peace through World Law.* Harvard, 1958.
9. See A. Martin and J.B.S. Edwards: *The Changing Charter.* Sylvan Press, 1955, pp.69 *et seq.*
10. B. Russell: *Common Sense and Nuclear War*, Allen and Unwin, 1959, and B. Russell: *Has Man a Future?* Allen and Unwin, 1961.
11. *Has Man a Future*, p.81.
12. *Common Sense*, pp.53 *et seq.*
13. The Manley-Brandt Report: *Global Challenge*, Pan, 1985, pp.176-7.

12: Perestroika: The Global Challenge

Stuart Holland

Until what seems like the day before yesterday, the prospects for global disarmament and development were bereft of any real chance of achievement. Today, the prospects seem entirely different.

The INF deal is a key to this change. What seemed only a hope at the time of NATO modernisation and the launch of the European Nuclear Disarmament Campaign, now is a reality. A superpower agreement to halve strategic nuclear weapons is on the agenda of feasible politics.

Against this 'summit scenario' the view from below is still unclear. The Iran-Iraq conflict threatens the stability of the Middle East. In its eleventh hour, the Reagan administration still is seeking to destabilise Nicaragua and restore its hegemony over Central America. The Soviet Union has set a schedule for withdrawing from Afghanistan, but still is involved in other zones of conflict such as the Horn of Africa.

Meanwhile, the SDI or Stars Wars initiative feeds the military-industrial complex in the United States — the self-same complex against which Dwight Eisenhower warned in the last speech of his presidency. Stockpiles of chemical and biological weapons have not yet been abolished. In Western Europe there are new calls for an independent deterrent, while NATO officials discount or deride the genuineness of new Soviet peace initiatives.

Nonetheless, the intent at the top to cry halt to the arms race is evident. In the Soviet Union, *perestroika* confounds the 'enemy image' of the 'Evil Empire'. The Soviet leadership wants to play a new role in the United Nations, build new links between COMECON and the European Community, and assist developing countries.

For the first time in decades, with a new agenda for both East-West and North-South relations, both disarmament and development are possible. The potential gains are immense. Yet the risks of failure also are formidable.

For one thing, the new disarmament scenario is being played against a background of major crisis rather than simply a perceived need for better co-operation. For the United States the crisis is international. Nuclear weapons have not defended America against dollar devaluation and the loss of its international economic hegemony. For the Soviet Union the crisis is mainly internal: the twenty years since the failure of previous reforms have seen scelerotic set-backs in output and productivity.

Likewise, the international market economy which, in the sixties, was still enjoying unprecedented economic growth, now itself is in recession. The developing countries are wracked by debt and the developed economies rent with unemployment. The Western model which seemed to combine both market freedoms and the security of a welfare society is itself in fundamental question.

If we do not understand the compound and often complex nature of such crisis, the window of opportunity for disarmament and development made possible by summit agreements may soon be darkened, if not closed.

The Challenge from the East
One of the key challenges for disarmament in the Soviet Union is how to achieve major change from military to civil production when the model of the civilian economy itself needs fundamental reform.

The scale of the challenge is well documented, by the Soviet leadership itself. Thus Mikhail Gorbachev has stressed that *perestroika* means both a political and economic restructuring of Soviet society. It means not only replacing administrative economic management with increased self-management, but also thereby a fundamental reform of the whole practice of 'democratic centralism'. It amounts to a revolutionary reform of the entire fabric of social and economic relations in the Soviet Union rather than a partial reform package.

But this poses key questions. How can the Soviet economy manage conversion from military to civil production without displacing labour and increasing open or disguised unemployment? If decentralisation is needed to increase efficiency, what role still needs to be played by central government in planning the resource shift from arms to civil production? Not least, can working people wait for benefits from such a major reform programme during a period in which they may see few direct gains in terms of their own income and welfare?

Sceptics abound, both within and without. Leonid Abalkin, Director of the Institute of Economics of the USSR Academy of Sciences, in an article in 1987 in the journal *Economics and*

Mathematical Methods (*Ekonomika i Matematicheskie Metody*), has argued that it is essential to introduce trade in means of production for reform to take off. Yet to do this now could be chaotic as a result of a combined supply shortage and excess demand.[1]

Alec Nove has claimed that there is a tension between the aims of *perestroika* as restructuring and the objective of *uskoreniia* or acceleration of growth, which demands greater attention to intensive development, to the quality of production and to consumer needs.[2] As Nove puts it, the dilemma is one in which it is impossible to do everything at once while at the same time contradictions arise if everything is not done at once. He argues that it is likely that *gozsakazy*, or state orders for production, will spread — rather than decrease as intended by *perestroika*. They could do so not as a result of central ministries seeking to reassert control, but because of

> "managers worried about shortages (and) about the unaccustomed task of actually finding customers striving to get as many of these compulsory state orders as possible".[3]

Likewise Mario Nuti has observed that there are many obstacles to reform. One of these is that "a reform is usually attempted in conditions of crisis, under great pressure, and this is the worst possible environment for the kind of reform that is being envisaged". Nuti notes that reform tends to be inflationary. It needs a certain breathing space, an improvement in terms of trade, a succession of good harvests, or — significantly — disarmament.[4]

Nuti also comments that a successful reform may initially worsen rather than improve economic performance, only followed later by an increase in efficiency and productivity. As he puts it:

> "We can expect fluctuations, further crises, and further reform campaigns until perhaps it will really happen. But there is one threat to the system, which is political. The system derives its legitimacy from economic success. Stagnation is bound to undermine its political legitimacy".[5]

Yet clearly Nuti sees scope for success. Also, he stresses that such success would amount to nothing less than the achievement of 'market socialism'.

Such market socialism rather than capitalist market relations, is the strategy for economic reform outlined by Abel Aganbegyan, chief economic advisor to Mikhail Gorbachev and key architect of the reform programme. As Aganbegyan puts it "market relations in the USSR are not of transient importance but part of the long-term development of a socialist economy". Also, in contrast with a capitalist market:

"Land and natural resources cannot be bought and sold. Since there is no unemployment and the economic basis of society accords with socialist ownership, there is no labour market. A market for capital is not envisaged as part of *perestroika*. There are no plans for a Soviet stock exchange, shares, bills of exchange or profit from commercial credit".[6]

Thus, while *perestroika* does mean market relations, it does not mean a restoration of capitalism, or a convergence with the capitalist market which dominates the US economy. In this sense, while elements of *convergence* may be discernable between the superpowers in terms of new market relationships, such convergence is by different economies and societies rather than simply from West to East.

However, such convergence could promote a key area for East-West co-operation and the economic underpinning of detente: international joint ventures. These joint ventures are not only advocated by Aganbegyan but also stressed as important by Mikhail Gorbachev.[7]

Such joint ventures can be either export promoting or import substituting. The recent declaration that the Soviet Union is planning to establish three major international economic zones on the Baltic, the Black Sea and the Pacific gives substance to the new proposals. The incentive is not simply foreign exchange, but also the transfer of technology from West to East in the civil sector of the economy.

At present such technology transfer is in large part blocked in key areas by the United States on grounds of military security. In other areas, the Soviet Union itself has pioneered new technology which it has licensed to Japan and other countries, without extensively applying it to its own industry.[8] Promotion of such joint ventures in entirely new sectors certainly should be a priority for Western European countries which are not prepared to accept a US veto on economic detente.

If the Soviet Union wishes to achieve an increase in foreign exchange through increased exports from its new economic zones, this in turn will depend in large part on sustained trade growth in the OECD countries. Yet at present such OECD export growth is only half that of the high period of the sixties and early seventies, and in no sense assures a global expansion during those years which the Soviets need to gain space and time for *perestroika* internally to succeed.

In the medium term, Soviet economists might well be advised to focus on import substitution through joint ventures rather than reply on export-led growth. Whether through foreign exchange saving or foreign exchange gaining, the net macroeconomic effect is the same. Meanwhile, such an inwards transfer of technology could assist in making possible the embodied innovation and raised productivity crucial to achieving higher income per head at home, and making feasible sustained conversion from armaments to civil production.

The Challenge for the West

If *perestroika* is a historic challenge for the Soviet Union, the United States and Western Europe need to restructure both their theory and practice in economic policy. In other words they also need 'revolutionary reforms'. If they fail to achieve them, they neither will be able to extend income and welfare nor defend themselves against economic decline.

At the time of Bretton Woods in 1944, the West had developed its own new agenda for society. In the United States, the New Deal had shown results in challenging the pessimism and limited self-interest of *laissez-faire*. In Britain, a new consensus had been established between the economics of Maynard Keynes and the social reform programme of Beveridge.

Problems remained — not least the overcoming of shortages of goods and foreign exchange. For some time, the challenge of surpassing recovery with sustained growth appeared as ambitiously unreal as some consider *perestroika* to be for the Soviet Union today.

Yet a new confidence pervaded the chancelleries and treasuries of the Western economies. Keynesian economic management through fiscal, monetary and exchange rate policy offered the prospect of full employment. The Beveridge reforms gave a framework for distributing gains from growth for distribution. Both meanwhile left the supply side of the economy predominantly in private hands.

Thus the Keynes-Beveridge formula appeared to offer a middle way between the excesses of a wholly planned or wholly unplanned economy. Throughout Europe for thirty years governments of Left, Right and Centre endorsed the main principles of what amounted to a new social, economic and political consensus.

Yet, by the mid 1970s, Keynesian demand management was undermined by the OPEC price hikes and rising unemployment. Economists such as Milton Friedman, upstaged during the Keynesian era, stepped forward with simple remedies for global crisis; reduce money supply and cut public spending, restore flexibility by wage cuts and float exchange rates. In short, re-establish primacy for profit and the private sector.

The monetarist counter-revolution had a simple appeal. In backing winners versus losers, it legitimated the self-interest which for most of the postwar period had been disguised behind consensus concern for full employment welfare programmes. Those ready to work, it was claimed, would price themselves into jobs, through lower wages. Anyone making money from a 'real job' in the private sector also could be a shareholder. Stripping public assets through privatisation both helped sustain profits and spread the illusion of a shareholder bonanza.

The bubble burst when stock markets crashed in October 1987. *Laissez-faire* and trusting markets — in an era of floating exchange rates — led to the lunatic consequence that whereas only a few years ago more than 85 per cent of foreign exchange transactions financed foreign trade, the same share, shortly before 'Black Monday', was financing speculation on future changes in exchange rates.

The crash has stalled the monetarist counter-revolution. But it has not yet ended the myth that unregulated markets provide the best of all possible economic worlds.

For one thing, conservative governments still are in office in key countries. Most of them are unwilling to change course. For another, the global crisis cannot be solved by going back to the kind of Keynesian policies which were part of the former postwar consensus. Put simply, the world has changed since Keynes. The main levers of Keynesian economic policy — exchange rates, interest rates and tax rates — have been dislocated by the rise of multinational capital on a global scale.

When Keynes wrote *The General Theory*, trade was predominantly international — between *different* firms in different countries. Today, it is overwhelmingly multinational — by or between the *same* firms in different countries. In a world where two hundred companies command a third of the global economy, traditional Keynesian exchange rate policies no longer can be relied on to stabilise world trade and payments or remedy the vast imbalance between the US and Japan.

Monetary policy and changes in interest rates still are important in affecting the cost of borrowing from building societies and banks. They also affect the freedom of manoeuvre for governments to shift savings into long-term government bonds rather than short-term stock market speculation. But interest rate changes no longer significantly affect decisions whether or not to invest in the big business sector which now dominates the industrial economies. This is essentially because they finance the overwhelming share of their investment needs through retained profits, and partly because their 'price-making' power enables them to offset higher interest rates by raising prices.

Likewise, fiscal policy no longer works as it was supposed to in textbook Keynesian models. The motor industry makes the point.

In the 1930s we had a British motor industry which sourced components from other British firms. Even US companies such as Ford and Vauxhall produced British models whose components were supplied by British industry. Now both components and production are overwhelmingly multinational, imported by US, European and Japanese firms from abroad. Thus lowering tax rates on car sales mainly increases imports rather than stimulating growth in the British economy.

Such changes in economic structures since Keynes mean that alternative economic strategies need to be international as well as national — combining joint action by key economies to reverse recession and promote global recovery.

For instance, it has been part of recent conventional wisdom — shared by many Keynesians and monetarists alike — that a cut in the US budget deficit, and thus US imports, would stabilise the dollar and settle world financial markets. This underlies some of the cross party pressure in the US Congress to get Ronald Reagan to cut the budget deficit by at least $23 billions this year and eliminate it altogether with a balanced budget by 1993. But in fact, such cuts could provoke a second financial crash since unless they are offset by expansion in other leading countries, they would steer the world economy from recession into slump, depressing profits and collapsing share values.

Essentially, one country's imports are other's exports. On projections from the model of the world economy available from European Federation for Economic Research, assumes progressive elimination of the federal deficit from 1988 till 1993 would cut US imports by two-fifths by the mid 1990s against their current trend rate of growth. In turn this could cut West Europe's exports by more than a quarter and raise Western European unemployment by up to six millions over the same period.

The impact of such cuts on Latin America's exports and ability to repay debt would be catastrophic. The fall in exports to the US could reduce Latin American growth by half from nearly 4 per cent last year to less than 2 per cent in 1989 and only 0.4 per cent by 1993 — a cut of over 10 per cent against the trend growth rate. This could trigger Latin American debt default and a threat to the viability of leading US and UK banks. In such a scenario, the lifeboat operation for the BP share issue would look like bandaid. Faced with the haemorrhage of major default, the Federal Reserve and the Bank of England either would shut their doors to have to intervene on a massive scale with moves equivalent to nationalisation of leading banks and discount houses.

It also is part of conventional wisdom to claim that the recent fall in the dollar should mean a recovery of US exports and a reversal of the massive US trade deficit. But no one should count on it. The dollar since 1971 has been devalued without improving US export performance. Over the same period, the Deutschemark and Yen have been successively revalued without eliminating their trade surplus.

The key reason is the dominance of US export trade by multinational companies. Through the 1970s and early 1980s more than three-quarters of US visible exports have been represented by multinational firms. At the same time more than half of total US imports recently have been from major affiliates or affiliated suppliers of multinational companies. But multinationals have little incentive to follow through the effects of devaluation with lower export prices in foreign markets where they are already producing and selling through their own subsidiaries. Put simply, why should IBM or General Motors compete against themselves on foreign markets?

Nor would a cut in US real wages, be sufficient to counter the Japanese export surplus. Although ignored by Thatcher and Lawson, the Japanese for years have combined guaranteed employment in their key export firms with high wages offset by productivity — increasing new technology. The labour content in the value of Japanese automobiles, engineering and electronics has for years been less than 10 per cent — and in some cases less than 5 per cent of the value of the product.

Clearly some US firms could respond to yet further dollar devaluation with lower prices abroad. Also, while leading Japanese firms have been able to offset revaluation of the Yen and the fall in the dollar in the last three years by major cost-reducing innovative investment, there could be some price for the dollar at which even Japanese profits would be squeezed — even if this does not eliminate the US trade deficit. It even has been suggested that this may be a tactic by some in the US administration who want Japan to join the Star Wars programme in a big way and see further falls in the dollar as the way to get them to agree.

Certainly the scale of the crisis in the western economies will increase the pressure for non-nuclear arms programmes, led by the US itself. The result could be both Star Wars and Trade Wars — destabilising yet further an already risk prone global economy.

Global Challenge: East-West and North-South

The pattern is classic — a militarist response to economic crisis which market forces cannot solve. But it must be resisted. If there is a meaningful and worthwhile cut to be made in the US budget deficit it should be in arms spending, matching the Gorbachev-Reagan agreement to remove intermediate nuclear weapons by making real a major reduction of strategic missiles.

If we are to transform the prospects for global economic co-operation — between both East and West and North and South — this must mean countering the logic of the Strategic Defence Initiative (SDI) with a new Disarmament and Development Initiative (DDI).

How could the US do this without destabilising its domestic economy through the spending cuts implied by an end to the arms race? How also can the rest of the world — or at least the world's leading economies — offset cuts in the US budget deficit in such a way as to counter deepening global crisis and a slide into slump?

First, the leading western economies should accept the call made in 1987 by US Treasury Secretary Jim Baker that they set recovery targets to expand their imports and make possible an increase in American exports. The addition to national spending by each country in the rest of OECD necessary to maintain a growth of 2.5 per cent a year in the industrial countries — thereby offsetting cuts in the US budget deficit by 1993 — is not unachievable. It would amount to an additional 1 per cent in both 1988 and 1989, rising to over 2 per cent by the early 1990s.

Second, the leaders of the western economies need to reschedule and restructure global debt. Simply through self-interest — to sustain their own exports — they should convene an international conference to reschedule debt repayment over a longer time period, limit interest rates on debt repayment and agree that repayment should not be more than a fixed share of export earnings — certainly not more than 20 per cent. Such a reform package would increase mutual spending and trade between the developed and less developed countries.

Third, the western economies need to defend and extend redistribution within the framework of re-mixed economy both to sustain demand and ensure that is matched by the long term investment supply which private markets will not ensure following the recent financial crash.

On the *demand* side, such redistribution means being able to restore public spending to promote momentum in mutual world demand and while regaining minimum welfare levels in housing, health, education and social services. In practice this means promoting social spending and income, not simply to increase welfare, but also to generate demand when the so-called 'wealth effect' — or less spending by the better off when the value of their shares has declined — otherwise would slow down the national and international economy. Shifting recovery through the pockets of the lower paid would help the process.

On the *supply* side, the western economies need to readmit the case for a remixed economy combining dynamism in both the private and public sector. This means countervailing the anarchy of private multinational capital in financial markets and establishing codes of conduct for the activities of multinational companies. Ideally, such codes should be reinforced by agreement on medium and long-term investment programmes of the kind which private speculation and buy-out share deals cannot ensure.

Such a new co-operation on trade and technology — including multinational public sector joint ventures — could in turn help support the process of liberalisation in the Soviet Union, Eastern Europe — and China. Examples of such potential are already available even at regional level in the UK.

Such a strategy amounts to the case for (1) recovery of global spending and trade; (2) a restructuring of debt and the mixed economy and (3) a redistribution of income and social welfare.

For instance, the case for international recovery, restructuring and redistribution as the premise for new international development has already been prototyped at the European level by the *Out of Crisis* project and by the Socialist International's *Global Challenge* programme.

The *Out of Crisis* report[9] was sponsored by the French Socialist Government, and provided the basis for the manifesto for the Confederation of Socialist parties of the EEC in 1984. The 1985 *Global Challenge* report[10] from the Socialist International — echoing the recovery, restructuring and redistribution imperatives argued in *Out of Crisis* — has been endorsed by more than eighty parties in as many countries, and attracted real interest from the socialist bloc and the non-aligned. The Chinese Communist Party and the Indian Congress Party attended the launch conference for the *Global Challenge* report at Lima in Peru in 1986.

The Soviet Union also have shown real interest in the report and its potential for global recovery. Mikhail Gorbachev has explicitly endorsed this approach by stating that:

> "The two parts of Europe have a lot of their own problems of an East-West dimension, but they also have a common interest in solving the extremely acute North-South problem . . . In this regard we share the spirit and thrust of the Brandt Commission's reports on the North-South issue and the report of the Socialist International 'Global Challenge' prepared under the guidance of Willy Brandt and Michael Manley".[11]

Crucially, both the US and the Soviet Union have joint interests in the triple challenge of recovery, restructuring and redistribution.

First, both superpowers have a vested interest in the means of achieving *recovery* of mutual spending, production, trade and income in the main OECD economies. The Japanese government has shown readiness to pursue such a recovery. But in the later 1980s real progress has been blocked by the triple conservative alliance of the governments of Britain, West Germany and France. The new Mitterand presidency and a socialist government could significantly change this.

Second, both superpowers need to *restructure* the supply sides of their economies and achieve a new industrial strategy. This is every bit as much the case for the US (though from a different base) as for the USSR. In the immediate postwar period the US did not need an industrial strategy because state intervention and public purchasing during the war had meant that it ensured a wide and diversified economic base with all industry cylinders firing in response to fine tuning of demand. Today, after nearly twenty years of Republican neglect, the US industrial base is dislocated and open to the highest foreign bidder.

Third, both superpowers need to *redistribute* resources on a major scale, from an economy in warfare readiness to an economy focused on the needs of civil welfare. Their starting points and their priorities clearly are different. The Soviet Union needs to move towards more consumer goods and services: it needs to personalise choice for citizens as consumers. The United States needs to socialise choice, not through socialism, but through making real the chance of equal opportunity for those in society who have been excluded from white, anglo-saxon, protestant and male privilege.

Such joint interests clearly mean moves towards a new model of development rather than old style growth in both the US and the USSR. They mean moving forward to a new agenda rather than sideways towards each other. They also imply new international and global imperatives rather than simply internal resolution of problems.

If there is a key concept for such progress towards a new international co-operation on disarmament and development it is clearly embodied in four words: A New Bretton Woods. The original Bretton Woods conference was sponsored by Roosevelt and influenced by Keynes. Yet it was inspired by something greater: the vision that the limits of the League of Nations and the force of nationalism could be transcended by a framework for genuinely international economic co-operation.

For reasons already argued in this text, the Keynesian basis for the old Bretton Woods has broken down. Joint action between nation states has been superceded in the market economies by joint dominance of multinational capital. The developing countries, then under colonial rule, were excluded from the first Bretton Woods framework. Crucially, the Cold War overtook the military and political co-operation of World War Two and excluded the possibility of real East-West co-operation after the war.

The next step for economic detente and co-operation, matching and supporting military detente, should include a New Bretton Woods conference, which addresses the issues confronting both East and West and North and South alike. Without *perestroika* and the new leadership in the Soviet Union such a prospect would be unreal. With it, and with an appropriate response from the new administration this year in the United States, it is as much on the agenda of feasible politics as has been the INF agreement and the prospect of a reduction of strategic nuclear weapons.

Clearly, the global imperative is to realign progressive parties and governments — in East and West and North and South — and to challenge the monetarism and militarism underlying the current crisis by an agenda for disarmament and development in the world economy. The costs of such a programme are a fraction of the risks of a global arms race. For instance, as well expressed in the *Global Challenge* report, a global recovery programme costing the equivalent of one-tenth of what the world spends each year on arms could make possible a genuinely new development decade.

If we choose not to work for disarmament and development in response to the present crisis, we then risk the fate against which Willy Brandt has warned — of 'arming ourselves to death'. For not only our own sakes, but those of our children, and their children, we have to build a new international order, into the twenty-first century, which can ensure human survival.

Footnotes

1. American Committee on US-Soviet Relations: "International Conference on the Gorbachev Initiatives", 29 October 1987, summary report, p.26.
2. *ibid.,* p.25.
3. *ibid.,* p.26.
4. *ibid.,* p.31.
5. *ibid.,* p.32.
6. Abel Aganbegyan, *The Challenge: Economics of Perestroika*, Hutchinson, London, 1988, p.127.
7. *Perestroika: New Thinking for Our Country and the World*, Collins, London 1987, pp.167, 183 etc.
8. Aganbegyan, *op.cit.,* pp.95-96.
9. *Out of Crisis*, ed. Stuart Holland, Spokesman Books, Nottingham, 1983.
10. Willy Brandt and Michael Manley, *Global Challenge*, Pan Books, 1985.
11. Gorbachev, *op.cit.,* p.196.

III

Common Action for Global Development

13: Socialist International Economic Committee: A Statement

The Economic committee of the Socialist International gathered in Portugal, at Estoril, in mid-April 1988. The issues with which this book is concerned were carefully discussed, and at the conclusion of the meeting, a declaration was approved. As will be seen, this declaration includes many of the specific ideas, and not a few of the actual words of the Disarmament and Development Appeal, which is featured in our introductory essay. We take this as evidence of new opportunities for co-operation and mutual aid. (Editor)

According to the new conventional wisdom, the market economies both have survived and surpassed the financial crash of October last year. Finance Ministers of the Group of Seven have just claimed that all is well in the best of all possible worlds, save for some minor adjustments needed in the prevailing international economic system.

The reality is very different. The world economy is at a crossroads. Some people in the developed countries seldom have had it so good. Personal income and wealth is high, while key sectors in such economies enjoy the prospects of sustained economic growth. But this disguises rising unemployment in the West and the crisis of drought, disease, deprivation and debt which currently cripples the South.

The current economic crisis increasingly divides the 'haves' from the 'have nots'. Summit complacency masks the scale of the problems facing developed and developing countries alike.

The US no longer can be the locomotive for the rest of OECD.

Most Western European countries have not reacted yet. The governments of Britain, France and the Federal Republic of Germany are "sitting it out": a doomed policy which will result in more unemployed and the real risk of a long and deep recession.

Japan is reacting, but it is difficult to assess to what extent and how fast it will redirect its economy to domestic needs. How much its trading partners will profit is equally uncertain.

Eastern Europe is in no better shape. the USSR is not only occupied with its internal restructuring but also has to contend with a diminishing income from its energy exports. Poland, Hungary and Romania are suffering from acute debt problems.

It is therefore more than necessary, particularly in Western Europe, to push forward expansionary economic policies. Public spending and redistribution of income to the lower income classes — instead of tax gifts to the well-to-do — are necessary to bolster private demand and public investment, for instance in housing, transport, new non-nuclear energy projects, etc. Tax changes should support real investment in the private sector and should no longer favour financial asset building and speculation in the merger and acquisition game.

It is clear that in the short term the debt problem cannot be solved by international growth alone. The Baker initiative is dead.

Inadequate action

The result is unbearable for many countries. This is now acknowledged by the new leadership of the International Monetary Fund (IMF), with its awareness of the need for internal growth in the indebted nations, and its insight that lower income classes in those nations need more to consume instead of more belt-tightening. But the IMF still is a net receiver of funds and not a giver. Overall, the South still continues to transfer resources to the North.

The World Bank, also is gaining new insight at the top, but still has not translated this into policies which avoid imposing negative conditionality on borrowing countries. It also lacks new capital. Its lending capacity for 1988 certainly will be below that of 1987. Efforts should be made to remedy this situation

The private banks are even less likely to provide fresh money. The internal cohesion of the banking consortia no longer exists. The Morgan deal with Mexico was not a success, not just because of its internal snags, but because the interests of US, European, and Asian banks, and between larger and smaller banks, have become too different to form new compromises. The only common denominator now is no new money.

Certainly awareness of the necessity for longer term solutions has grown. There is a greater willingness to come to real long term agreements and there is now a common — albeit not always open — acknowledgement that debt and/or interest must be forgiven. The questions are: how much, under what terms and who organises it? The so-called market is rather a limited indicator for this because it is not well organised, it deals only with marginal sums, and most importantly, it normally gives no relief to the indebted countries. It is therefore not surprising that private banks now increasingly ask for political solutions and political leadership.

Clearly there are measures which must be taken by the debtor countries, especially on taxation, trade concessions and support in the fight against capital flight. It should not be forgotten in this context that the creditor countries are the recipients of most of the flight capital.

Export credit by industrialised countries is both too low and too slow. Also such credit mainly supports export promotion in the developed countries regardless of development needs. Bilateral aid needs to be put on a grant rather than loan basis, and increased.

Global Recovery

The priorities today for common action and cooperation lie in initiatives made by the developed countries. Especially, the leading OECD countries should set targets for the recovery of their spending and trade.

Last year US Treasury Secretary Jim Baker called on the leading OECD governments to set targets for the recovery of their own economies and take the strain off the United States. They failed to do so. Such failure contributed to the stock market crash of October 19, 1987.

Since the crash, Finance Ministers in the Group of Seven have talked of exchange rate targets but done nothing to ensure the sustained growth of mutual trade which is critical for stability in the world economy.

Such policies result in a beggar-my-neighbour deflation of global trade. For instance since 1981, the Latin American countries have reduced their imports by two fifths in order to generate the foreign exchange to repay debt. But in so doing, they have reduced exports from the developed countries.

Recovery by the leading OECD economies would sustain and increase developing countries export trade.

Debt Restructuring

But recovery programmes also must be accompanied by a rescheduling and writing down of a major part of the multilateral, bilateral and commercial debt of the least developed countries.

The present grave situation cannot continue since it is a major barrier to economic growth and undermines democracy in the debtor countries. It also creates instability in the international banking system. The case by case approach of restructuring and the menu of partial relief measures. e.g. debt equity swaps, have not and cannot resolve the debt crisis. A multilateral political consensus must be forged among the governments of creditor countries, commercial banks, multilateral institutions and the debtor countries. All share the responsibility for creating the problem and must share in the resolution.

The debt of developing countries is similar to the historic war debt of European countries — but with a crucial difference; the new debt derives from a war on poverty rather than on peoples. It should be restructured on a basis similar to that applied to European debt after World War II. Those terms included rescheduled repayment over at least thirty years and cancellation of some debt.

Such new measures of debt relief must be accompanied by increased financing for the adjustment process. The proposed expansion of the Compensatory Financing Facility, CFF, will provide additional financing. But it will include increases in interest rates and involves conditionality. This is a reversal of the guiding principle of automatic dispensation under the CFF. This does not address the problem of reducing the outstanding stock of debt.

A meaningful solution must be based on the following six principles:

1. Conversion of discounted debt to long term bonds through a new facility within the IMF/World Bank or a new institution.
2. Cancellation of the major share of the debt of the least developed countries.
3. Interest rates ceilings and the limitation of debt services to a reasonable share of export earnings, related to the development needs of the countries concerned.
4. Increased funding for and lending by the IMF and the World Bank, including Special Drawing Rights and new credit flows, possibly using IMF gold reserves as collateral.
5. Dispensation of CFF funds with minimal conditionality.
6. More appropriate conditionality, longer periods of adjustment in IMF programmes and the Structural Adjustment Facility of the World Bank, and an enhanced role for the international Labour Organisation in the elaboration of complementary social and labour market policies.

Redistribution and Environment
Redistribution is crucial to global recovery. Debt and deflation impoverish the peoples of the developing countries. They also prevent the welfare policies which are crucial to sustaining programmes in housing, health, education and social services, as well as reducing those resources which are needed to defend a sustainable environment.

The issue of debt and the environment gives a striking example.

Economists for generations have claimed that air is a free food. Yet key developing countries have been cutting into the tropical rain forests which service the world's oxygen through their imperative to find any means available to service their international debt. If the international community is to take seriously the recommendations of the Brundtland Report on the global environment, it will allow such countries relief on debt in order to preseve the environment crucial to our global survival.

This again implies a redistribution of resources. But such redistribution also is imperative in the developed countries in order to make possible a sustained recovery. The slow-down in economic growth in the OECD is only partly due to the OPEC oil price increases of 1973 and 1979. It is in larger part due to the relative saturation of demand at prevailing and unequal levels of income distribution. Put simply, we cannot sustain global economic growth merely by giving more to those who already have in sufficiency or to excess while the majority of the world's population lack more than the bare minimum necessary for survival.

Technology and development
Global distribution also concerns the new multinational division of capital, labour and technology

New technologies are transforming the growth prospects of advanced sectors in the developed countries. But they also threaten to devastate the future export income of less developed countries. These countries recently have suffered a massive loss in the terms on which they trade with the rest of the world. This now is compounded by negative effects for them from the application of new technologies.

Radical technological change such as flexible automation is undermining the comparative advantage of low labour cost countries in international trade. New bio-technologies mean that it soon will be possible for developed countries to produce the agricultural products which — since the early 19th century — were assumed by most economists to be the preserve of the developing countries. The prospect that Europe, the US and Japan can supply themselves with such products through these new technologies is devastating for the prospect of the poorer countries.

If new technology is to liberate rather than constrain the Third World, this in turn implies that the international community must address the issues of technology transfer to and autonomous technical capacity for the developing countries themselves.

The UNCTAD code on transfer of technology already provides a framework for progress in this area, and its adoption would be an important step in this direction. Meaningful negotiations on the new GATT Round will depend in large part on such progress.

Multilateral Action

The post war framework of multilateral institutions has proved incapable of meeting the global challenge of development. It also has been marginalised by unilateral action. In particular, the US Administration over the last seven years has not agreed to any outcome of the North-South negotiations, whether the Common Fund, new or renewed commodity agreements or the Law of the Sea convention which itself is so crucial in particular to preserving the rights of developing counties to off-shore minerals. It not only has withdrawn from UNESCO, but also has refused to recognised the international Court of Justice verdicts on Central America, has rejected a minimally adequate replenishment of IDA funds, and has attempted to relegate IFAD, the FAO and UNCTAD to virtual insignificance.

The US with other critics may be right in claiming that change in the character and format of North-South negotiations are necessary. But to plead for improvements in multilateral agencies is one thing. To withdraw from or undermine them without creating a viable alternative is entirely different.

Clearly we do need reform of the UN framework itself. More than forty years after its foundation, with the massively wider membership of the former colonial countries, there is a strong case for restructuring multilateral institutions. Informal groups, whether in groups of five, seven or 24 or more, cannot easily cope with the range of problems confronting the international communities.

South-South cooperation is of paramount importance to achieving a genuinely new international economic order. In this context, we strongly welcome the establishment of the South Commission under the chairmanship of Julius Nyerere.

We also recommend a widened role for the Economic and Social Council of the UN and a clear reestablishment of its authority over the policies pursued by key agencies such as the IMF and the World Bank. Such agencies should not be seen simply to serve the interests of top countries and top companies in the global economy.

Further, the authority intended originally for the International Trade Organisation should be reestablished in relation to the programme of GATT in such a way as to ensure that freer trade does not simply represent greater freedom for big business to dominate small countries, but contributes to social progress, improved working conditions and increased employment.

Lomé III will expire in 1989. Negotiations on Lomé IV will start this year. From the perspective of global development, it is of the utmost importance that Lomé IV provides more financial aid; an enlargement of the STABEX fund; reduced protectionism and improved market access for processed agricultural products, as well as support for regional development.

Crucially new multilateral initiatives to reform the international monetary system are needed for:

1. the provision of an IMF intervention capability in foreign exchange markets, on the basis of reserves contributed by the US, Europe and Japan;
2. a major increase in the issue of special drawing rights to improve international liquidity;
3. increased private and public use of the European currency unit, thereby promoting a global system based not only on the dollar and the yen, but also the ECU;
4. the matching of a system of target zones for the main exchange rates with targets for the recovery of OECD trade.

Like-minded action

Reacting to the dispersal of power in multiple UN agencies, many countries have evolved their own regional forms of economic cooperation. Some such groupings have failed to achieve their main objectives, such as the Latin American Free Trade Association. Others such as the European Community still are dominated by problem sectors in transition such as agriculture, but have shown potential for genuinely autonomous development.

Nonetheless, such regional groupings as the European Community are not homogeneous. The EC so far has failed to promote the recovery programme crucial to ensuring that the OECD countries can offset slower growth in the US economy. The combination of conservative governments in Britain, France and West Germany obstructs such a recovery programme. Yet Europe has the possibility — and should take responsibility — to promote measures to recover spending, income, trade and jobs which would both benefit its own people and those of the developing world.

It is imperative that like-minded governments in the international community take joint action to confront the global economic crisis. This means in practice that they not only should press the case for recovery, restructuring and redistribution in regional and multilateral institutions, but also should achieve a common framework for action to promote such objectives on a global scale.

The feasibility of such common action has been illustrated by the programme of the Nordic countries jointly to fund development assistance to the SADCC countries in Southern Africa. Such a programme could well be extended with the cooperation of other countries to other regions of the world.

Not least we need to admit the global opportunities made

possible by the opening of new perspectives for international joint action with the Soviet Union and China. For too long international action has been limited to the agenda of the market economies of the West. We now should respond more clearly to the restructuring and new openness which is occuring in the East.

Disarmament and Development

On such a basis there are genuine prospects for building both an East-West and North-South dialogue which can realise the hopes for both disarmament and development.

Until recently the prospects for global disarmament were bereft of any real chance of achievement. Today, the prospects seem entirely different. The INF deal is a key symptom of this change. A superpower agreement to halve strategic nuclear weapons now is on the agenda of feasible politics.

The intent at the top to cry halt to the arms race is evident. Nonetheless, the process has only just begun. Stockpiles of chemical and biological weapons have not yet been abolished. The Iran-Iraq war threatens the stability of the Middle East, while the African and Asian subcontinents are rent with wars which lacerate their prospects for development.

Massive conventional weapons still are deployed in the First, Second and Third Worlds alike — preempting development spending in such areas as housing, transport, health, education, social services, and the environment.

The priority now is not only to make progress on specific arms reductions, but also to advance the case of disarmament *for* development. The international peace movement — and the recent response to Band Aid, Live Aid and Sport Aid — mobilised millions of people worldwide against hunger and in support of disarmament and development.

But hitherto, even when they have drawn support from the same people, these causes have remained separate. We must bring them together, because unless the world is made fit for its peoples to live in, peace will always be in jeopardy: and while the world's treasure is wasted on war preparations, poverty and distress will always recur.

In this context, we cannot afford the extension of the arms race by either superpower into space. The world does not need the SDI of a Strategic Defence Initiative. It desperately needs the DDI of a Development and Disarmament Initiative, including both East and West and North and South. If we do not achieve this, as Willy Brandt has stressed, we risk "arming ourselves to death".

Afterword

Ken Coates

Andre Gunder Frank has reminded us that the Chinese ideograph for "crisis" is made up of an amalgam of two other characters. One of these is the word "danger". The other is the sign for "opportunity"

There is danger enough in the present world. No-one can read the Brundtland Report without feeling that danger very directly. Even when we ignore the perils of military confrontation, the cost of industrial "progress" is already fearful, and may soon become unendurable. Our common future, if future we have, must rest on a degree of international co-operation scarcely imagined by our most cosmopolitan forebears.

A great new alliance of democrats will be necessary if such co-operation is to become practical and effective. Many old divisions will have to be overcome. Harmful intolerances and irrelevant dogmas will need to be abandoned, and a new tolerance and trust will have to take their place. Maybe it all seems too much to ask, too far to reach. Are we not seeking the key to enter utopia?

Utopia may frighten the realists among us and it has certainly become an unfashionable location in recent times. Perhaps it may remain so in the future: but there is no question about one thing: the idea of the future is unbearable without the existence of hope. While hope has been thought to be a Utopian notion, futurology has become more and more despondent. Suddenly, in the late eighties, this is no longer true. Even while the problems accumulate, people begin to feel the stirring sense that, by joining together, perhaps, just perhaps, we can do something about things.

That is why we are sure that the discussion so imperfectly entered in these pages will grow and develop. In its light, we shall begin to see the limits of danger and the scope of opportunity.

Appendix

International Conference on Relationship between Disarmament and Development

New York, 24 August-11 September, 1987

The International Conference on the Relationship between Disarmament and Development concluded three weeks of meetings on 11 September 1987 at UN Headquarters with a reaffirmation by participating States of the international commitment to allocate a portion of the resources released through disarmament for socio-economic development, so as to bridge the economic gap between developed and developing countries.

States agreed to consider reducing the level and magnitude of their military expenditures to and use existing regional and international institutions to reallocate resources released through disarmament, and to accord priority to the allocation, through the United Nations, of part of such resources for emergency humanitarian relief operations and critical development problems.

The Conference's Final Document, adopted by consensus, recommends an action programme to foster an interrelated perspective on disarmament, development and security; to promote multilateralism in those fields; and to strengthen the central role of the United Nations in the interrelated fields of disarmament and development.

The Document further states that, considering the present resource constraints of both developed and developing countries, reduced world military spending could contribute significantly to development. Disarmament could assist the process of development not only by releasing additional resources, but also by positively affecting the global economy. It could create conditions conducive to promoting equitable economic and technological co-operation and to pursuing the objectives of a new international economic order.

In concluding remarks, the Conference President, Natwar Singh, Minister of State for External Affairs of India, said the international community had, by an overwhelming majority, agreed that there existed a close and multi-dimensional relationship between disarmament and development. It was incomprehensible that such a relationship should be denied in some influential quarters. The adoption of the Conference Final Document by consensus, he added, was yet another step in the direction of arresting the retreat from multilateralism that had been witnessed in recent years.

After adoption of the Final Document, statements were made by the representatives of Denmark (on behalf of the 12 members of the European Community), Canada, the German Democratic Republic (on behalf of the socialist States), Mexico, the United Kingdom, France, Algeria, Sweden, Australia, the Netherlands, the Federal Republic of Germany, New Zealand, Zimbabwe, China, Switzerland, Egypt, Japan, Costa Rica, Finland, Libya (on behalf of the African Group), Cameroon and Morocco.

While most delegations welcomed the consensus adoption of the Final Document and viewed it as a victory of multilateralism, many said it was a compromise text which failed to completely satisfy their concerns.

Mexico, for example, regretted that the document did not contain any proposal for the future establishment of a fund to channel the resources freed by disarmament measures towards development in developing countries. The socialist States also believed that a special mechanism for the transfer of part of the resources released through disarmament to developing countries would ensure the required institutional relationship between disarmament and development. They further suggested that the Security Council should consider the relationship between disarmament and development at the highest level.

Mexico, Zimbabwe and others believed that the document attached an exaggerated importance to the concept of security. It indicated, they believed, a preference for the concept of security put forward by the major military alliances, to the detriment of the system of collective security envisaged by the Charter. Sweden, on the other hand, believed that the document interpreted security in the broadest possible political, economic and human sense.

Zimbabwe also said that the Final Document, instead of focusing primarily on disarmament by those States whose military expenditures had the greatest effect on the world economy, had been drafted so that it could be interpreted to mean that the arms expenditures of the smallest countries were to be treated like those of the most powerful. China also regretted that the Document did not place the primary responsibility for disarmament on the superpowers.

On the other hand, the United Kingdom stated that by devoting so much attention to defence expenditures in the industrialised world, the Document ignored the high military budgets and the question of arms production in many developing countries. The United Kingdom further stated that the document failed to reflect the need for transparency in the provision of estimates on military expenditures. It also declared that if any savings materialized from disarmament measures, it reserved the right to allocate those in accordance with its own priorities through the channels it deemed most appropriate.

The Netherlands, together with the United Kingdom, said that they could not accept the economic analysis contained in the Document, which pointed to the military expenditures of the industrialised countries as the main cause of problems in the world economy.

France said the Final Document did not address the real problem of the relationship between disarmament and development. The implementation of disarmament had to take into account various facts including the question of stability of States. Also, the links between the relieving of defence burdens and financing of development projects could not be seen as a cause-and-effect link.

Final Document
The States participating in the International Conference on the Relationship between Disarmament and Development.

Desirous of:

(a) Enhancing and strengthening the commitment of the international community to disarmament and development and giving impetus to renewed efforts in both these fields;

(b) Raising world consciousness that true and lasting peace and security in this interdependent world demands rapid progress in both disarmament and development;

(c) Directing global attention at a high political level on the implications of world-wide military spending against the sombre background of the present world economic situation;

(d) Looking at disarmament, development and security in their relationship in the context of the interdependence of nations, inter-relationships among issues and mutuality of interests;

(e) Taking greater account of the relationship between disarmament and development in political decision-making;

(f) Furthering the international community's collective knowledge of the military and non-military threats to security;

Adopt the following Final Document:

1. In the Charter of the United Nations, Member States have undertaken to promote the establishment and maintenance of international peace and security with the least diversion for

armaments of the world's human and economic resources. The Member States also express in the Charter their determination to employ international machinery for the promotion of the economic and social advancement of all peoples. The United Nations has thus a central role to play for the promotion of both disarmament and development.

2. Disarmament and development are two of the most urgent challenges facing the world today. They constitute priority concerns of the international community in which all nations — developed and developing, big and small, nuclear and non-nuclear — have a common and equal stake. Disarmament and development are two pillars on which enduring international peace and security can be built.

3. The continuing arms race is absorbing far too great a proportion of the world's human, financial, natural and technological resources, placing a heavy burden on the economies of all countries and affecting the international flow of trade, finance and technology, in addition to hindering the process of confidence-building among States. The global military expenditures are in dramatic contrast to economic and social underdevelopment and to the misery and poverty afflicting more than two-thirds of mankind. Thus, there is a commonality of interests in seeking security at lower levels of armaments and finding ways of reducing these expenditures.

4. The world can either continue to pursue the arms race with characteristic vigour or move consciously and with deliberate speed towards a more stable and balanced social and economic development within a more sustainable international economic and political order; it cannot do both.

5. Global interest in the relationship between disarmament and development is reflected in proposals by a politically and geographically broad spectrum of States since the early days of the United Nations. There is an increasing understanding of this relationship, in part due to the expert studies and reports prepared by the United Nations.

6. The contrast between the global military expenditures and the unmet socio-economic needs provides a compelling moral appeal for relating disarmament to development. There is also a growing recognition that both overarmament and underdevelopment constitute threats to international peace and security.

7. The convening under the aegis of the United Nations of the International Conference on the Relationship between Disarmament and Development is a landmark in the process of undertaking, at a political level, the multilateral consideration of the relationship between disarmament and development.

Relationship between disarmament and development in all its aspects and dimensions

8. While disarmament and development both strengthen international peace and security and promote prosperity, they are distinct processes. Each should be pursued vigorously regardless of the pace of progress in the other; one should not be made a hostage to the other. Pursuit of development cannot wait for the release of resources from disarmament. Similarly, disarmament has its own imperative separate from the purpose of releasing resources for development.

9. However, disarmament and development have a close and multidimensional relationship. Each of them can have an impact at the national, regional and global levels in such a way as to create an environment conducive to the promotion of the other.

10. The relationship between disarmament and development in part derives from the fact that the continuing global arms race and development compete for the same finite resources at both the national and international levels. The allocation of massive resources for armaments impedes the pursuit of development to its optimal level.

11. Considering the present resource constraints of both developed and developing countries, reduced world military spending could contribute significantly to development. Disarmament can assist the process of development not only by releasing additional resources but also by positively affecting the global economy. It can create conditions conducive to promoting equitable economic and technological co-operation and to pursuing the objectives of a new international economic order.

12. Real economic growth as well as just and equitable development, and particularly the elimination of poverty, are necessary for a secure and stable environment at the national, regional and international levels. They can reduce tensions and conflicts and the need for armament.

13. In the relationship between disarmament and development, security plays a crucial role. Progress in any of these three areas would have a positive effect on the others.

14. Security is an overriding priority for all nations. It is also fundamental for both disarmament and development. Security consists of not only military, but also political, economic, social, humanitarian and human rights and ecological aspects. Enhanced security can, on the one hand, create conditions conducive to disarmament and, on the other, provide the environment and confidence for the successful pursuit of development. The development process, by overcoming non-military threats to security and contributing to a more stable and sustainable

international system, can enhance security and thereby promote arms reduction and disarmament. Disarmament would enhance security both directly and indirectly. A process of disarmament that provides for undiminished security at progressively lower levels of armaments could allow additional resources to be devoted to addressing non-military challenges to security, and thus result in enhanced overall security.

15. An effective implementation of the collective security provisions of the Charter of the United Nations would enhance international peace and security and thus reduce the need of Member States to seek security by exercising their inherent right of individual or collective self-defence, also recognised by the Charter. The judgement as to the level of arms and military expenditures essential for its security rests with each nation. However, the pursuit of national security regardless of its impact on the security of others can create overall international insecurity, thereby undermining the very security it aims at promoting. This is even more so in the context of the catastrophic consequences of a nuclear war.

16. It is widely accepted that the world is overarmed and that security should be sought at substantially lower levels of armaments. The continued arms race in all its dimensions, and its spreading into new areas, pose a growing threat to international peace and security and even to the very survival of mankind. Moreover, global military spending on nuclear and conventional arms threatens to stall the efforts aimed at reaching the goals of development so necessary to overcome non-military threats to peace and security.

17. The use or threat of use of force in international relations, external intervention, armed aggression, foreign occupation, colonial domination, policies of *apartheid* and all forms of racial discrimination, violation of territorial integrity, of national sovereignty, of the right to self-determination, and the encroachment of the right of all nations to pursue their economic and social development free from outside interference constitute threats to international peace and security. International security will be guaranteed in turn to the extent that peaceful and negotiated solutions to regional conflicts are promoted.

18. Recently, non-military threats to security have moved to the forefront of global concern. Underdevelopment and declining prospects for development, as well as mismanagement and waste of resources, constitute challenges to security. The degradation of the environment presents a threat to sustainable development. The world can hardly be regarded as secure so long as there is polarization of wealth and poverty at the national and international

levels. Gross and systematic violations of human rights retard genuine socio-economic development and create tensions which contribute to instability. Mass poverty, illiteracy, disease, squalor and malnutrition afflicting a large proportion of the world's population often become the cause of social strain, tension and strife.

19. Growing interdependence among nations, interrelationship among global issues, mutuality of interests, collective approach responding to the needs of humanity as a whole and multilateralism provide the international framework within which the relationship between disarmament, development and security should be shaped.

Implications of the level and magnitude of the continuing military expenditures, in particular those of the nuclear-weapon States and other military important States, for the world economy and the international economic and social situation, particularly for developing countries

20. The current level of global military spending in pursuit of security interests represents a real increase of between four and five times since the end of the Second World War. It also reflects approximately six per cent of the world gross domestic product and has been estimated to be more than 20 times as large as all official development assistance to developing countries. During the 1980s, global military expenditure has grown on an average at a faster rate than during the second half of the 1970s.

21. The bulk of global military spending remains concentrated among some developed countries that also carry out almost all the world's military research and development. It has been estimated that global expenditure on military research and development represents approximately one-quarter of the world's expenditure on all research and development. During recent years, as weapons have become more sophisticated, the rate of increase in spending on military research and development has been higher than the general increase in military expenditures.

22. The military sector also consumes a significant proportion of world energy resources and non-energy minerals and diverts skilled human resources and industrial production, which could be utilized in other sectors. Moreover, the production and stockpiling of armaments, particularly of nuclear and chemical weapons, poses a significant threat to the environment.

23. While arms exports are dominated by a number of developed countries, the developing countries account for a major share of arms imports. The adverse development implications of such transfers outweigh immediate trade benefits to the supplies and

security gains to the recipients.

24. In contrast to the current level and trends in global military expenditure, the state of the world economy in the 1980s has been characterised by a slow-down in growth of demand and output compared with the preceding two decades, generally lower rates of inflation, difficulties in many countries in adapting to structural changes, a mounting stock of debt, high real interest rates, inadequate net flows of financial resources, shifts in exchange rates, high and increasing levels of protection, commodity prices depressed to their lowest level in 50 years, terms-of-trade losses sustained by commodity exporting countries, and a generally insecure economic environment in which millions of people still lack the basic conditions for a decent life.

25. The use of resources for military purposes amounts to a reduction of resources for the civilian sector. Military spending provides little basis for future industrial civilian production. Military goods are generally destroyed or soon used up. While there are some civilian by-products of military research and training there are better direct, non-military routes to follow.

26. The opportunity cost of military expenditures over the past 40 years has been and continues to be borne by both developed and developing countries, as there is a pressing need for additional resources for development in both groups of countries. In developing countries, it has been estimated that close to one billion people are below the poverty line, 780 million people are undernourished, 850 million are illiterate, 1.5 billion have no access to medical facilities, an equally large number are unemployed, and 1 billion people are inadequately housed. In developed countries, resources are required, *inter alia*, for meeting the priority needs of urban renewal, the restoration of some of the infrastructures, the reduction of unemployment, the protection of the environment, the further development of welfare systems and the development of non-conventional sources of energy. The developing countries are doubly affected: (a) in proportion to the expenditure they incur themselves; and (b) because of the disturbing effect of military expenditure on the world economy.

27. The present world economic situation should also be seen in the context of the arms race. For certain countries the high deficits caused by military expenditures as well as the cumulative effect of subsequent rise in the interest rates have the effect of diverting substantial flows of capital away from development activities. In this sense, the whole world is affected by the arms race.

28. Moreover, military-related production tends to be capital-intensive, usually creating fewer jobs than would result if an equivalent amount of public funds had been spent on civil projects.

Inefficiency associated with the non-competitive conditions of the military market-place has a negative effect throughout the economy, including productivity and cost, and on its competitive position in the international market.

29. Global military expenditure has an impact on the world economy through interdependence among nations and the interrelationship between the global macro-economic variables. Attempts at understanding the present world economic situation and attaining stable and sustainable growth need to take account of the current levels of military expenditures.

Ways and means of releasing additional resources through disarmament measures for development purposes, in particular in favour of developing countries

30. Apart from promoting international peace, security and co-operation, disarmament can improve the environment for the pursuit of development by:

(a) Releasing resources from the military to the civilian sector at the national level;

(b) Removing the distortions in the national and international economy induced by military expenditure;

(c) Creating favourable conditions for international economic, scientific and technological co-operation and for releasing resources for development at the regional and international levels, on both a bilateral and a multilateral basis.

31. Resources released as a result of disarmament measures should be devoted to the promotion of well-being of all peoples, the improvement of the economic conditions of the developing countries and the bridging of the economic gap between developed and developing countries. These resources should be additional to those otherwise available for assistance to developing countries.

32. The release of additional resources for the civilian sector is in the interest of both industrialised and developing countries, as it would mean the stimulation of economic growth, trade and investment. Among developed countries, this could also mean additional resources to meet pressing socio-economic needs, while in the developed countries it could contribute to the achievement of the goals of social welfare. However, working towards the release of resources through disarmament is not enough; an international development strategy is a vital stabilising element in international relations.

33. The disarmament dividend may be obtained in a variety of forms. These could include trade expansion, technological transfers, the more efficient utilisation of global resources, the more effective and dynamic international division of labour, the

reduction of public debt and budgetary deficits, and increased flows of resources through development assistance, commercial and other private flows or transfers of resources to the developing countries.

34. Past experience has shown that conversion from military to civilian production need not present insurmountable problems.

Action programme
35. With a view:

(a) To fostering an interrelated perspective on disarmament, development and security;

(b) To promoting multilateralism as providing the international framework for shaping the relationship between disarmament, development and security based on interdependence among nations and mutuality of interests;

(c) To strengthening the central role of the United Nations in the interrelated fields of disarmament and development:

(i) The States participating in the International Conference reaffirm their commitments in the fields of disarmament and development and reiterate their determination to adopt, both individually and collectively, appropriate measures to implement these commitments. These will include bilateral, regional and global initiatives for peaceful resolution of conflicts and disputes;

(ii) They also stress the importance of respect of the international humanitarian law applicable in armed conflicts. Respect of this law makes it easier to pave the way for a solution to conflicts, and hence ultimately to release resources for development;

(iii) They recognise the need to ensure an effective and mutually reinforcing relationship between disarmament and development and to give practical expression to it through specific measures at the national, regional and global levels;

(iv) They reaffirm the international commitment to allocate a portion of the resources released through disarmament, for purposes of socio-economic development, with a view to bridging the economic gap between developed and developing countries;

(v) In this connection, they will give further consideration:

a. To the adoption of measures to reduce the level and magnitude of military expenditures which, in addition to being an approach to disarmament, would be a means of reallocating additional resources for social and economic development particularly for the developing countries;

b. To the utilisation of existing regional and international institutions for the reallocation of resources released through disarmament measures for socio-economic development, particularly in developing countries, taking due account of existing capabilities of the United Nations system;

c. To accord priority to the allocation, within the framework of the United Nations, of part of the resources, including human and technical resources, presently devoted to military purposes for emergency humanitarian relief operations and critical development problems, pending the achievement of genuine disarmament under effective international control;

d. To the importance of greater openness, transparency and confidence among nations with a view to facilitating progress in both disarmament and development;

(vi) They will consider:

a. Keeping under review issues related to a conversion of military industry to civilian production and undertaking studies and planning for this purpose;

b. Undertaking studies to identify and publicise the benefits that could be derived from the reallocation of military resources;

c. Making the results of experience in, and preparations for, solving the problems of conversion in their respective countries, available to other countries;

(vii) a. To continue to assess their political and security requirements and the level of their military spending, taking into account the need to keep these expenditures at the lowest possible level, and to keep the public informed on the subject;

b. To assess the nature and volume of resources that may be released through arms limitation and disarmament measures and to consider including in future disarmament negotiations provisions to facilitate the release of such resources;

c. To carry out regularly analyses of the economic and social consequences of their military spending and to inform their public and the United Nations about them;

d. To appeal to appropriate regional organisations and institutions to carry out, within their mandates as appropriate, analyses of the political, military and economic factors in their regions, with a view to encouraging regional measures of disarmament and development;

(viii) They recognise that an informed public, including non-governmental organisations, has an invaluable role to play in helping to promote the objectives of disarmament and development and creating an awareness of the relationship between disarmament, development and security. They therefore agree to take appropriate measures to keep the public informed in this regard;

(ix) They emphasize the need to strengthen the central role of the United Nations and its appropriate organs in the field of disarmament and development, in promoting an interrelated perspective of these issues within the overall objective of promoting international peace and security;

    a. The United Nations and the specialised agencies should give increased emphasis, in their disarmament-related public information and education activities, to the disarmament-development perspective;

    b. They request the Secretary-General of the United Nations to intensify his efforts to foster and co-ordinate the incorporation of disarmament-development perspective in the activities of the United Nations system;

    c. The United Nations should make greater efforts to promote collective knowledge of the non-military threats to international security;

    d. An improved and comprehensive data base on global and national military expenditures would greatly facilitate the study and analysis of the impact of military expenditures on the world economy and the international economic system. To this end, the broadest possible number of States should provide objective information on their military budgets to the United Nations according to agreed and comparable definitions of the specific components of these budgets. In this connection, the work under way in the United Nations for a systematic examination of various problems of defining, reporting and comparing military budget data should be intensified;

    e. The United Nations should continue to undertake, on a regular basis, analysis of the impact of global military expenditures on the world economy and the international economic system. Consideration should be given to the idea of establishing a mechanism within the existing framework of the United Nations to monitor the trends in military spending;

    f. The United Nations should facilitate an international exchange of views and experience in the field of conversion;

    g. The General Assembly, in receiving the report of this

Conference, is requested to keep under periodic review the relationship between disarmament and development in the light of this action programme, including its consideration at the forthcoming third special session devoted to disarmament.

Contributors

Michael Barratt Brown, a director of the Russell Foundation, is an adult educationalist (founder of Northern College) and a specialist on the economics of development. He is the author of *After Imperialism, Essays on Imperialism, Models on Political Economy* and numerous other works.

Keith and Anne Buchanan, are well known for their writings on *The Transformation of the Chinese Earth* and the *Geography of Hunger*, and are regular contributors to ENDpapers. They are presently living in New Zealand.

Luciana Castellina is a Member of the European Parliament and the Central Committee of the Italian Communist Party. She is one of the founders of the European Disarmament Movement.

Ken Coates is Reader in Adult Education at Nottingham University. He is a member of the Bertrand Russell Peace Foundation, and editor of Spokesman publications.

Andre Gunder Frank is Professor of Economics at Amsterdam, author of *The European Challenge* (Spokesman, 1985) and many other works on development studies.

Mikhail Gorbachev, general secretary of the Soviet Communist Party, addressed this open letter to the United Nations on the occasion of its 42nd General Assembly. It was subsequently published in *Pravda* on September 17th. Since it offers a remarkably succinct statement on the new thinking in the USSR, we invited a cross-section of western socialists to offer their own responses to it.

Stuart Holland is a Labour Shadow Minister for Treasury and

Economic Affairs. He edited the *Out of Crisis* report (Spokesman, 1983) and has recently published *The Market Economy* and *The Global Economy* (Weidenfeld).

Rt. Hon Neil Kinnock is leader of the British Labour Party.

Marek Thee is a senior research fellow of the International Peace Research Institute, Oslo, and editor of its quarterly journal, the *Bulletin of Peace Proposals*.

Maarten Van Traa, former international secretary of the Dutch Labour Party, is now a member of parliament. *Bob de Ruiter* is assistant to the Labour Group in the Dutch Parliament.

Joop den Uyl, former leader of the Labour Party in the Netherlands, prime minister and distinguished spokesman of the Socialist International, died last December. He will be very much missed by socialists and democrats all over Europe.

Norbert Wieczorek. An SPD economic spokesman in the Bundestag, Norbert Wieczorek was a member of the European team which prepared the report on socialist economic co-operation, *Out of Crisis*.